Revisiting John Dewey

Revisiting John Dewey

Applying What He Said 100 Years Ago to Today's Need

Latasha D. Holt

ROWMAN & LITTLEFIELD
Lanham • Boulder • New York • London

Published by Rowman & Littlefield
An imprint of The Rowman & Littlefield Publishing Group, Inc.
4501 Forbes Boulevard, Suite 200, Lanham, Maryland 20706
www.rowman.com

86-90 Paul Street, London EC2A 4NE, United Kingdom

Copyright © 2023 by Latasha D. Holt

All rights reserved. No part of this book may be reproduced in any form or by any electronic or mechanical means, including information storage and retrieval systems, without written permission from the publisher, except by a reviewer who may quote passages in a review.

British Library Cataloguing in Publication Information Available

Library of Congress Cataloging-in-Publication Data

Names: Holt, Latasha D., 1983– author.
Title: Revisiting John Dewey: applying what he said 100 years ago to today's need / Latasha D. Holt.
Description: Lanham, Maryland: Rowman & Littlefield, 2023. | Includes bibliographical references. | Summary: "This book provides a glimpse into today's school system. Readers are challenged to question the school's purpose through a more human lens"—Provided by publisher.
Identifiers: LCCN 2023004105 (print) | LCCN 2023004106 (ebook) | ISBN 9781475869842 (cloth) | ISBN 9781475869859 (paperback) | ISBN 9781475869866 (epub)
Subjects: LCSH: Dewey, John, 1859–1952. | Education, Humanistic. | Education—Philosophy. | Education—Aims and objectives.
Classification: LCC LB875.D5 H65 2023 (print) | LCC LB875.D5 (ebook) | DDC 370.11/2—dc23/eng/20230224
LC record available at https://lccn.loc.gov/2023004105
LC ebook record available at https://lccn.loc.gov/2023004106

*To my children Chloee, Haylee, & Blakelee,
Nana & Daddy,
and Mom,
for whom this book was written.*

To one of the greatest supports as I was writing this book.

Thanks to each of you for being my biggest fans.

Contents

Foreword	ix
Preface	xi
Acknowledgments	xv
Introduction	xvii
Chapter One: The Purpose of School	1
Chapter Two: Children at the Center	19
Chapter Three: How We Teach	39
Chapter Four: Curriculum	59
Chapter Five: Futuristic Needs	73
Chapter Six: Preparing Teachers for the Future	93
References	111
About the Author	113

Foreword

Having grown up in the classroom as a teacher's kid, we got a rare perspective the rest of the world doesn't see. Watching our mother work her teacher magic over the years, we have seen the incredible impact a teacher has on the world around them. This book captures the heart of our mother and so many other teachers just like her.

What makes this book unique is the combination of personal stories and foundational facts regarding our educational system and the changes that would make it better. What we learn, how we learn, and who we learn from has an important impact on students' lives and the future of our world. We will grow up one day to be leaders ourselves.

This book emphasizes the important role that teachers and a supporting community play in the future of democracy.

This book shares an in-depth viewpoint into an educator's life and the many struggles they must overcome.

This book promotes the good works of a teacher in our society and paves a way for other educators who can strive to be the best they can be for the whole child.

This book provides a gateway for the schools and the community to unite.

Being a student in today's world is no easy task. So much time is spent working and studying to further our education. Someday if we have children of our own, we hope our educational system has taken a word from our mom and all others who have devoted their time to speak about this cause.

We are each grateful that we got the opportunity to watch our mom dedicate so much of herself to meeting the needs of her students and families for so many years. Now, we have had the chance to watch her move through the stages of writing this book. This book is truly an inspiration to all of us.

—Chloee, Haylee, and Blakelee

Preface

"Learn all you can. Your education is something that no one can take from you."

—Dad

I shadowed a 1st-grade teacher my senior year of high school. I was about to start college, and I wanted to make sure teaching was the right career path for me. I still remember walking into that elementary classroom and sitting quietly in a tiny chair in the back. The teacher was teaching a reading lesson, and I was amazed.

As soon as I watched her, I knew that what I saw happening was something special. Now I realize that something special was teacher magic. From that day on, I knew working in education was what I wanted to do with the rest of my life.

I went on to graduate high school and attend college. For the next 4 years, I learned under the best professors and instructors. I finished a degree in early childhood education and set out to change the world.

I got my first teaching job at a high-needs school. Typical teacher life happened right away. After getting the keys to my classroom, it was clear to see that the teachers I would be working with were tired and frustrated. I observed first-hand the effects of low teacher morale.

Next, I met my students and quickly realized they were struggling too. Many of my students were trying to persevere academically despite facing hardships. They faced food insecurities and home lives full of abuse and neglect. Most lacked access to the academic resources they needed to be successful.

Soon after I reached my 2-year teaching milestone, I decided to pursue my master's degree in education. I hoped that learning more would better equip me to meet the needs of the students and families I served. My studies focused on curriculum and instruction. This degree emphasized reading, special education, and teaching English as a second language; all these areas were in high need.

While continuing to teach, raise a family, and study, the reality hit. It began to sink in just how broken education is. Year after year, I remained frustrated with policies and procedures that made no sense. From the very start of my teaching career, I had students who were abused, homeless, neglected, and without the basic resources needed to learn. Since schooling mostly focused on academics, I had somehow been programmed to believe that the business of dealing with basic needs was for someone else.

Being fair, not all was bad. There were a few initiatives to help students sprinkled here and there. We had a food backpack program that sent backpacks of food home for the weekend. The students helped pack the food and deliver it to classrooms every Friday.

The food backpack program became very important to me. One Monday morning, a student of mine explained to me his weekend meals consisted of ketchup and mustard. He explained that ketchup and mustard had to do for his meals because it was all they had in his house left to eat. From that Monday on, I made sure each weekend a food backpack was sent home for him and his family.

Monday through Friday, daily breakfasts and lunches are not free in public schools. For several of my students, getting a hot meal was not an easy task. Some may have qualified for the free and reduced breakfast and lunch program. If the student's family met the income guidelines and returned completed forms, children could be approved to receive a warm meal at a lower cost. Even though I have yet to understand why children must pay lunch money to eat at school, the free and reduced lunch program was a supportive option.

The paying for breakfast and lunch expectation has always bothered me. In America, children who are required to attend school by law are not always guaranteed a meal. I, like many other educators, personally paid for many lunches for my students so they could eat hot food like their peers.

In addition to nutritional support, students' mental health needs were recognized. Identified students were serviced using partnerships between the local counselors they saw outside of school and the school they were attending. Counselors would pull out the students they served a couple times a week from our class. Often, the students would sit with their counselors in a room down the hall. Sometimes they would play board games while catching up. Board games are a great way to teach students about the basics of winning and losing. They are also a great way to make time for conversation.

One day something clicked. Our classroom was the place the counselors were needed. The students they were working with needed more assistance when interacting with peers during real class time and not so much in isolation. After that, I began to encourage counselors to stay with our entire class and support the student directly in the environment which they were a part of.

Looking back, I believe it was about year eight of my teaching career that I began to burn out. I never told anyone I was tired or burned out; it was just something I strongly felt. The feeling deeply bothered me. Despite all the things my school and district had going on to support student needs, so much more needed to change. I was exhausted, and I did not see a way to solve all the stressors I was bearing. I swore to serve these people.

I decided pursuing a PhD in curriculum and instruction would allow me to continue to serve in education but in a different way. This degree would allow me to qualify for a job in higher education. A job in higher education would allow me to reach others beyond my one single classroom.

In my new role, I would exponentially help pour into preservice teachers. They would go on to take my place in education and together change the lives of hundreds of children and families. I could use my knowledge and experiences to impact hundreds of future teachers. After earning a PhD, I did just that. For the past seven years, I have been researching, publishing, and enjoying my time in a higher education position. I work every day with teachers and future teachers who are changing the world!

Each day I continue to grow as a human being. I have come full circle, and yet the same desire to change the world is still in me. I have realized that in the world of education, things are still broken. There are still educational policies that make no sense. Despite the challenges, I must continue to be an advocate for education.

Looking forward there is so much work to be done. Education is *broken*. Now, more than ever, teachers are quitting, children are in need, and parents are at their wits ends. School systems are broken and backward. Likewise, policy and home environments are broken. Educators are exhausted and our communities are extremely divided.

The greatest educational philosopher and my personal educational hero is John Dewey. Counting back, it was over 100 years ago when Dewey told us we needed to reset education. During his lifetime, Dewey spoke often of education, democracy, and social needs. Dewey made it clear through his over 1,000 publications and numerous lectures that without reform our democracy is at stake. He devoted over 70 years of his life sharing his message across the world.

Despite Dewey's extensive work to change education, year after year, we have continued to do the same things over and over. We systematically avoid conversations about the root causes of the issues we face in education. We continue to do a huge disservice to our children, families, teachers, and community.

For the past year, my personal mission has been to be an active listener to others. I want to come up with a solution to the problems we face in education. To make a change, it is important to deeply engage with what others are telling us using their words and actions. Using facts and critical thinking, I have formed some big conclusions. These conclusions, and the work of John Dewey, have helped me write the content of this book.

This book is for educators and administrative leaders at all levels across the globe. This book is for scholars, politicians, parents, and other members of our community. We can no longer blame teachers, parents, bogus laws, bad children, or bad curriculum. We must now take responsibility and stop the finger pointing at each other. The lives of our children, grandchildren, and the future of our democracy is on the line. For these reasons, this book is full of comparing, sharing, and giving a voice to the voiceless.

Acknowledgments

I would like to thank my three girls who have given their unwavering support through this process; thank you, Chloee Holt, Haylee Holt, and Blakelee Holt. You each have supplied me with extra love and encouragement.

To one of the greatest supports when this book was written. You were a pillar of strength I leaned on and were an invaluable source of encouragement.

To Nana Paulette Reynolds, I owe so much. She gave her time to read the manuscript at all of its stages. The honest feedback she shared kept me excited to complete this book and share it with the world. To my father, Rodney Reynolds, you have always been my rock. I appreciate all the advice. To my mother, Rebecca Reynolds, thank you for sharing your ideas and reassurance.

My students inspire me. Thanks to each of my students for letting me learn with you. You are our hope for change. To my colleagues both past and present, thank you for your guidance and encouragement. To Tom Koerner, my editor, this would not be possible. I give a special thanks to Tom and the team who helped me share my heart in the pages of this book.

I know each of you are so proud of me.

Introduction

"Education is not preparation for life; it is life itself."

—John Dewey

Education across the globe is in a crisis. Teachers are quitting at record rates. Children are struggling both academically and socially. School shootings are on the rise. Parents are frustrated, and our businesses are struggling to hire and keep workers. What has happened to our educational system and community. How will we ever overcome the challenges?

Just this past May, Uvalde, Texas, became home to the deadliest school shooting in the United States in over a decade. Nineteen students and two teachers were killed by an active shooter. The shooter was only 18 years old. It was difficult to watch television or scroll through the trending TikToks about the shooting. The children killed were fourth graders. Having taught fourth grade for many years, it was all too personal. Many times, throughout my career, I had sat in active shooter professional development training and thought through what I would do if I was in a situation like this. I wondered if these teachers who were killed defending their students had sat in similar trainings and wondered about the same things as me.

I am now a college professor. In this role, I prepare preservice teachers and closely work with other experts to help our educational community grow. As a college professor, some of the most difficult days were having to face a classroom full of preservice teachers the day following a mass school shooting. One shooting tragedy I can recall was the Parkland High School massacre.

I vividly remember heading to work at the University the day after the Parkland High School shooting. It was February 15, the day after the 19-year-old student entered his high school and began shooting. The boy had been expelled from school after getting into trouble. In total, 17 people were killed that day. *This past summer, I had the chance to hear from a*

Parkland High School student who survived the shooting event. Hearing her speak was solemn but made me hopeful for the future.

I remember trying to sort out my own thoughts on the drive to work that day. Ultimately, I decided it best to scratch my normal plans to cover reading fluency assessments, and instead I would facilitate a sit and talk time about the mass shooting tragedy that was flooding the news. I reminded the class that our home state of Arkansas had faced a school shooting in the late 1990s. I tried to give some hope that we were a little more prepared for this type of violence in our area.

I shared other specific facts I hoped would ease their minds. I explained that in my elementary teaching position, I was provided active shooter training. I encouraged them to advocate and participate in similar trainings when they had their own teaching jobs. I shared that the schools in our area had special locking doors making access to most schools a one-point entry. This level of protection was in place to make it more difficult for a shooter to get inside.

I discussed the built-in door barricades that were installed in each classroom for the entire school district sometime after the Sandy Hook Elementary shooting. This barricade was a heavy upside down "u" rod with one side that could slide into the brick wall and the other side into the heavy metal classroom door. When in place, this made entry to my classroom almost impossible. Each day I made sure that heavy piece of metal was propped next to the door in case it was needed. These barriers were in place to protect our class.

I went on to share details of the kid-friendly school safety lesson I taught to my 4th graders. My lesson explained to the young students that they should walk behind me in line and listen for good directions in times of need. I used the analogy that our class was like a big duck family. I told the young students I was the parent duck, and they were my ducklings. I explained it was my goal to keep them safe as best as I could. I never chose to use the word "shooter" to my fourth graders. Inside my heart, I knew that this duck lesson would be helpful whatever may come our way.

Next, I facilitated a talk time where the preservice teachers shared their personal thoughts about the deeper causes of violence in the world. A few examples that were shared and discussed included monitoring playground time and dealing with school bullying. I explained that anger-filled moments on the playground, and in other school settings, could grow into anger-filled acts of violence played out later in life.

I challenged them to think of teachable moments that could help a student heal any issues they may have with others in the school community instead of holding on to anger and choosing to do harm. Using different scenarios, I facilitated modeling activities with some Conscious Discipline thinking strategies. We left campus that day with the conclusion that this was a topic we did not have all the answers to.

As I shared, I could not watch the live news footage of the most recent Texas school shooting. However, I did catch the shooter's name and a picture in the transcripts of an interview. I learned that the shooter's social media was being investigated and was involved in the timeline leading up to the shooting. I wanted to draw my own conclusions, so I decided to search the personal Instagram page of the shooter. There it was. Several warning signs were right in front of me and the rest of the world.

Next, I searched for a second interview about the Ulvade shooter. According to the article, the grandfather of the shooter explained the gunman (his grandson) was living with him and his grandmother after a "falling out" with his mother. The grandfather was unaware that his grandson had guns, and he indicated that he, the grandfather, had a criminal record himself and was not allowed to have guns. He explained that if he would have known about any guns, he would have reported it to the authorities.

When asked about the school his grandson chose to attack, he said that his grandson had not been to school this year. He shared that he was a very quiet kid. I learned that just before the shooting at the school, the shooter shot his grandmother in the face. I also learned that at the elementary school he attacked, his grandmother worked there as a teacher's aide.

Before this tragic event, I wish someone would have questioned why the shooter hadn't been to school himself all year. I wonder if a home visit from his teacher and principal would have made a difference. Maybe he had been at that school with his grandmother sometimes. Was that connected at all?

I want to know his school story. The truth is, we may never know the details. Hurt people, hurt people. We need to better understand the roles that schools play in these situations. We should be proactive, not reactive. The following chapters challenge us to think more deeply about the role of schools in creating solutions to school issues so that we can be proactive together.

John Dewey believed that education should not be separate from our societal needs. The content in this book revisits the foundational work of John Dewey that he shared almost 100 years ago. Dewey had much to share regarding the state of education, and its connection to our larger society. One caution he illustrated throughout his life was that without educational reform, our democracy would be at risk. Despite his warning, education is still functioning much like it was so long ago.

This book includes six chapters that each analyze key ideas from John Dewey's work that are still applicable to our world 100 years later. By connecting Dewey's foundational ideas to today's educational system, we can begin to unite as a community and organize a better plan to address our educational challenges. We can learn so much about what changes should take place once we identify the basics that are lacking in our current educational system which have begun to affect our shared society.

To meet the goals of this book, a focus is given to the basic educational needs that we should address. This includes:

- revisiting the purpose of schools
- refocusing on the need for children to be at the center
- addressing how we teach
- addressing the 100-year-old curriculum debate
- strategically planning for future educational needs
- preparing our teachers

Each of the chapters are set up with three parts. Each begins with an overview, followed by connections to Dewey's thoughts related to current educational issues. Each chapter ends with a summary challenge to help us begin to analyze what we are doing in our schools and classrooms that does not make sense. As you read, you will see many connections across the chapters. You may read a chapter and choose to re-read another. The chapters contain details with stories and purposes that are all unique, but overall, each chapter connects to the others.

Using current, real-world examples that align with the basics, we can finally begin to move education in the direction it should have been going 100 years ago. If John Dewey could speak to us today, this book provides insight on what he might say, and without change, why the future of our democracy is in trouble.

Before beginning to read this book, take a moment to write down what you believe the purpose of school is for. Keep this written idea close and refer to it often as you read the chapters. I challenge you to take each page of this book and refer to your purpose of school. Ask yourself and others if what we are doing day after day makes sense for the present life and the future of democracy. Brainstorm ways you can help make a change. Big or small, we must all do our part to make this world better.

Chapter One

The Purpose of School

"The school must represent present life."

—John Dewey

OVERVIEW

This chapter introduces John Dewey and shares his thoughts on the purpose of schools. He challenges society to get back to the basic human needs. Through Dewey's writings and lectures, he shared a great deal about what he believed the purpose of school should be. He also shared his societal concerns and gave recommendations for needed change.

Schools, in Dewey's vision, were more than just places students would receive subject-specific content knowledge. School systems should not be thought of as a separate part of society. The needs of society and ensuring the students develop subject-specific content knowledge must be recognized as one and the same.

Dewey believed that schools are primarily social institutions. Dewey explained that our schools must represent the present life. Schools should be real life and hold important value to the needs of students. The way the school is structured and functions, should align with the lives carried on in the home, in the community, or on the playground. He explained that these social institutions were critical to the longevity of democracy and the only way to truly teach subject-specific content knowledge.

The idea of schools functioning as a place for social growth brings about so many questions to think about. Schools should not restrict the social parts of development to meet hundreds of subject-specific content standards. But that's what is happening.

Schools cover hundreds of content standards each year. There are standards for math, reading, science, writing, social studies, and more. These standards are taught and assessed in classrooms, in district modules, and on state standardized tests. We must decide if today's schools are structured in ways that serve the social growth for children. If they are not structured for social growth, how can we make changes?

It is possible that there is a lack of shared understanding of how important social development is in today's schools. Perhaps this is why we have a foundational problem with education needing to be addressed. If the purpose of schools is to serve as a meeting ground of students where:

- social needs lead the way
- real-world knowledge is obtained
- subject-specific content information is developed
- democracy lives on

Then why do we continue to waste so much working in the wrong direction?

Who Is John Dewey?

You might be wondering who John Dewey was. John Dewey remains widely accepted as one of the greatest educational philosophers of all time. Dewey spent his entire adult life thinking about philosophy, education, and our society. He spent his days writing and lecturing about his educational discoveries. Having lived from the Civil War to the Cold War, he saw great changes in the world unfold. His life gave lots of societal changes to think about.

Dewey wrote 37 books and published 766 articles in 151 journals. He taught for nearly 40 years at universities in Michigan, Minnesota, Chicago, and at Columbia in New York. Dewey was internationally known for both his work in philosophy and education. He traveled internationally to African, Asian, and European countries where he extended his educational influence. He even had a lab school.

As shared, Dewey was passionate about society, so he advocated for the rights of women, children, and diverse people. He spoke out about war, economics, and schooling. Dewey believed that democracy is more than a form of government, it is a form of society.

Because Dewey spoke of difficult issues like discrimination, war, equality, and politics, his work became a target for criticism. His beliefs about schooling were criticized for being too free and out of proper order. Despite his work being criticized at times, Dewey patiently defended himself. He reminded his educational followers that students should not be allowed to do whatever they please. Planning and organization must accompany freedom. Teachers should be guides of social thinking needs and subject matter experts.

According to Dewey, children should be given authentic opportunities to grow their subject-specific content knowledge with a purposeful connection to their own lives. After all, students' own individual lives are part of a larger community. If the school systems are purposeful, they can serve as the pipeline of knowledgeable, young citizens that will grow up to lead in the functioning society to which they belong.

Authentic opportunities to gain knowledge come by ways of making connections to real life. This looks different than what we see in today's schools. Think about real life. Whether real life be an appointment at the doctor's office, a dinner party, shopping, or traveling, true opportunities in *real* situations are where education begins to happen. Schools, at their best, are fake simulations that seem boring and unimportant. If the students we are teaching are bored and have no care to learn, we are stuck . . . period! Our schools are not living up to their societal purpose, and we need change.

Evolving Schools

It was a lecture given in 1899 and eventually published, that John Dewey encouraged us to think about school, the home, and neighborhood community in a new light. With the start of the industrial revolution, things were changing. The student's household, that was practically the center or the means where all things with daily life happened, had changed, Dewey explained.

Before the industrial revolution, all family members' participation was needed to make the household function. To survive, the household had to function in an efficient manner. By function, we must think of the most basic human needs that had to be acquired. These needs included things like food and shelter.

To have enough food to eat and a warm home in the winter, each person had a role and specific jobs to do. Hunting, canning, cooking, and chopping wood are not a one-person task. It took many people coming together to get things done. The need to survive year after year led to a strong, central family community. This central community had all members of the household society participating and fostered a sense of pride and belonging.

It was 15 years before World War I when Dewey made the declaration that the days of the past were ending. He knew the way daily life had been was changing. He cautioned that society should recognize the shift in daily lives and embrace the new ways community and schools would need to evolve. Dewey did not say community would go away, but that community, as it had been understood would change.

We are now living 125 years later and the educational community has yet to fully embrace the changes in society and seek to understand the connections to real world needs. Another perspective to consider is that we are now living five generations later than when Dewey gave his call for a declaration of change!

Today, our lives are full of technology that is used in almost everything we do. Yet our schools struggle to embrace technology, its place in the community, and its role in the daily lives of the present and future. This struggle to embrace technology is seen with school policies and common procedures that prohibit technology use such as cell phones. If students are caught with a cell phone, often disciplinary actions are taken.

There is a lack of concern to provide technology training for teachers and students. There is a lack of advanced technology tools for students and teachers to access, *and* there is the sad reality that more technology is being used to order a meal at a restaurant drive-thru than in most classrooms! Our industrialized, technology-driven world that we must learn to live in has made the required daily life tasks and communication more convenient. This evolution has also made a world independent from any direct human contact at all. Yet schools continue to forbid the use of technology and choose to remain behind.

Despite advancing and modernizing times 125 years later, including the impending metaverse and the Walmart drone delivery pilots, it remains that children still need to grow with the changes of their lifetime. Children still need a community of belonging. Our school communities have not changed or evolved with the basic needs of students. Today's students need to be technology ready members of society that have value and belonging in their communities. Our schools are behind and need to catch up.

Dewey understood that schools, even at their best, would be no match against the happenings in the world. Therefore, it is important that schools and society should function as one rather than be in a competition with each other. If school is left to compete with the world, the world will win. Dewey knew that teachers would become overwhelmed trying to engage students. Students will not connect their lagging behind school day content to their more advanced out-of-school life.

While you might think this information seems obvious, the reality is that day after day, schools keep doing things the way they have always been done and no one really questions it. This is another educational hurdle that we must face and challenge for school structures to change. We need a systematic, deep-rooted change to be developed, organized, and implemented.

Some of the industrial revolution advancements that Dewey talked about are now commonly used in today's everyday life. It is important to question in what ways the school has connected to the changes in society to prepare students to thrive. There are new innovative changes today's students now deal with in their real lives.

The Purpose of School

A friend in high school did not care to graduate. He saw no purpose for the extra stress in his life since he was all set to take over his family farm. He saw no connection of school to his world. A lack of connection between the advances of farming things related to food production is harmful. Schools should connect and set meaningful learning goals.

Consider This Example:

Much of America is farmland. The U.S. Department of Agriculture shared that in 2021 there were 2,012,050 farms in America. Farms, big or small, are important for the basic need to obtain food. Farmers, wanting to grow large amounts of corn, can use a GPS tool to map the field. This mapping technology can be applied to computer programs that estimate the amount of corn that will be produced. This estimate allows farmers to plan what "extras" they might add such as water and fertilizer and what the result would be.

Because of this farming technology, a more accurate cost analysis report can now be produced and help the farmer better plan for the season's work. Then the combine tractors can be programmed to basically drive themselves in the fields to harvest using the GPS technology data. School might have been more engaging for the young farmer if the real-world applications had been connected to it.

Food technology is just one of the many developments since World War I. Cars that can drive themselves without a human in the driver's seat can be purchased. Apps connected to small robots on wheels can deliver take-out food to your door. Robotic arms can be fry cooks in a fast food restaurant. Drone technology is a huge part of military advancements used to be more effective in combat and keep soldiers safe. Even the simpler daily chores like vacuuming the floor are now being accomplished with the help of advanced technology.

Searching for jobs online, you might find a job listing looking for cabots to employ. Cabots are robots that work beside humans. We must ask, "do our schools support teachers to create opportunities that prepare students to be cabots?" The future of jobs, like the ones that have a need for cabots, are not the focus of educational decisions being made. Many schools lack access to the most basic computers for each student to use.

Schools are systematically not designed to continually keep up with the fast pace of the world. Without change, schools will continue to seem pointless to students. Students are consumed with the important task of trying to survive their real lives that are in a much-advanced outside world.

The report *A Nation at Risk* was shared with the U.S. Secretary of Education in 1983. This 2-year in-depth study of America's educational system was a directive to uncover the state of education. The report shared that the public recognized that something was missing in our educational system.

In the report, it was shared that the public-minded citizens that participated shared their concerns (at their own expense) and should be recognized for their honest information.

It was the Cold War that was the real concern. The space race and news of the Sputnik launch caused a post-haste reaction to focus on issues with the current educational system in the United States. Even the U.S. military reported educational trends that were alarming. The military was concerned the country was at-risk since students were graduating high school with a lack of basic educational skills. If you read the report and the findings that were a call for change, the issues we face today are still the same since 1983.

Dewey worked with schools in Chicago. Dewey shared his observation that thousands of young children were practically ruined at the hands of the public schools each year. Understanding that most classrooms do not look and function anything like the society that we want to live in, and that our students are academically behind, leads to an unhelpful solution of finger pointing. Maybe finger pointing makes us feel better believing that someone else is to blame for the lack of positive direction in education.

Who is to blame? It depends on the context. Often the case is that teachers suggest more parent involvement is needed to remedy the educational issues we face. On the flip, parents often think the school system and members of the school community are at the root of the problems and should be held responsible. Some think that students have changed for the worse. The truth . . . we are all responsible.

To resolve the challenges we face, we must first look inside our homes and communities for gaps that must be filled. It is important to realize that these gaps are not just with subject-specific content knowledge that can advance the economy. The human element is important. Education can improve the human conditions. Addressing human needs can change education. Remember, societal and educational needs are symbiotic.

The filling of identified gaps should start with the child's basic needs and building their sense of belonging. A child's role in the greater society matters a great deal. Any gaps in basic needs or their importance to society need to be identified and addressed. Teachers and school systems cannot do this alone. It will take all members of the society being involved.

While the purpose of school is to educate and prepare students to be functioning members of their society, the ways in which the school functions should be revised. Schools cannot be anti-democratic and isolated from the world. Schools are such a big part of helping children develop, build morals, character, and learning the best ways to manage their life and learning.

As Dewey stated, "when the school introduces and trains the child of society into membership within such a little community, saturating him with the spirit of service, and providing him with the instruments of effective self-direction, we shall have the deepest and best guaranty of a larger society which is worthy, lovely, and harmonious." Sadly, tiny, productive communities are not the case in most classrooms.

Students are lacking with basic needs and sense of community. The way schools are structured seems like there is no help in sight. The lack of basic needs being met leads to bigger problems for health, citizenship skills, and stagnates the job market. The lack of a strong foundation causes students to avoid participation in school. Often, this leads to crime, and the goal of transitioning knowledge comes to a halt.

We must continue to question the purpose of schools and their progress to evolve with the changes life brings. We must be involved and keep each of the moving pieces in check. Teachers must be allowed time to nurture and authentically make plans for the needs of their students. Without expecting teachers to nurture and plan, Dewey said that it would be a crime against our democracy.

Children are the people who make up the school. The school's primary role is to meet the needs of the children. Some believe it is solely the teacher's job to meet all the child's needs. It takes more than just the teachers.

Some will say the teachers are not alone. But the actions from members of the community do little to help. Society continuously allows teachers to bear all the burdens of meeting the needs of each child by themselves.

The school needs supporting members. The members should consist of more people than just teachers, administrators, school board members, and a few volunteers. The help that teachers need consists of more than just extra supplies (although help with basic supplies is always a plus). Teachers need a community with a plan that systematically asks and listens to needs, and then brings all the community's best talents and resources to them.

As shared, teachers need more than school supplies. Needs consist of a continuous flow of clothes, meals, health check-ups, and mentors. The teachers need supporters that ask how things are going and follow up with support. This support can be:

- helping meet needs as an ally
- a political sounding board
- community initiatives for homes and families.

Teachers have never been given this kind of continuous support. At best, the support has been hit or miss.

The school is the community. The community is the school. Dewey shared his belief that much of present day education fails because it neglects the fundamental principle that the school is a form of community life. There should be a new coined term for a new type of school. In this new school, it must be made clear that no one is alone. All hands are helping.

Perhaps the new term for what use to be called a school should be community-centered school. Changing the name can be a sign to the world that the old ways of doing things has passed. Community-centered schools include the typical school leaders, children, parents, and all members of the larger community. The new meaning of a community-centered school must be widely known and accepted by all members of society as a new improved model of education.

The new school model should function the same way a thriving community does. These types of communities are seen during a storm or when someone in the neighborhood loses everything in a house fire. These are communities that face a need of great magnitude and come together to give so freely, listen, offer their own talents, and check back the next day . . . ? The community-centered school needs a community with a spirit like the ones we see come alive in times of great tragedy.

A community-centered school should be the place for all societal needs to be understood and addressed together as one. There is a joke about becoming a teacher meaning you are becoming a teacher, nurse, mom, counselor, food source, and a problem solver. While it is true that teachers do take on many of these roles, one teacher cannot do all the work alone. The old saying "it takes a village to raise a child" is actually a better example of how a community-centered school of experts must unite.

Without being united, from a single teacher perspective, supporting every student's needs can seem like an impossible task. For one teacher alone, this pressure can be quite unbearable and cause burnout over time. There must be a systematic way to ask, identify, and intervene to meet the needs of students in today's school systems.

When the basic needs are met, then the desire to pass on content knowledge and a strong sense of community can flourish. How will we see the change? Dewey said change will happen when the community understands the moral responsibility to help educate. The lack in resources needed to help teachers and students will no longer be an issue. Time, attention, and money will be at the disposal of the teacher.

Schools and Basic Human Needs

In a classroom setting, teachers can have 20 plus students at one time. It can take months of school to get to know each child on a personal level. It can take a long period of time before a teacher realizes that a student is lacking basic needs and should reach out to the community for help.

It takes time to build rapport between the child and their caregiver. The school day does not factor in time for teachers on a regular basis to do student wellness check-ins. School counselors and nurses are spread thin trying to meet the needs of the entire school population at once. Often these school counselors and nurses are frustrated themselves and feel overwhelmed. When no help is available, teachers step in. The heartaches teachers face by themselves must be recognized and given support.

Recently assigned to a classroom observation placement at a local school, a preservice teacher interacted with a third grader in a one-on-one group setting. The third grader had been meeting regularly with the preservice teacher twice a week for about three weeks. The student was getting extra support with her writing skills. Preservice teachers often spend time in schools to gain classroom teaching experience before entering the final teacher residency. Both the preservice teacher and child benefit from the time spent working together.

On this particular occasion, the preservice teacher was observed chatting with the third grader while working over a small dry erase board with magnetic letters. Quickly the preservice teacher looked away from the child and was seen wiping tears from her eyes.

Later it was shared that during that small meeting, the third grader had explained that both of her parents were dead due to gun violence. Not knowing this important detail about the child's life devastated, shocked, and saddened the novice educator. Often preservice teachers discover the realities of a child's home life struggles in random situations like this.

It would be helpful to know more about situations that children face from the start. Having this knowledge can help to address the emotional needs a child has alongside the content planned for the day. Unfortunately, outside of school, home situations are not always a part of the daily classroom conversations between students and teachers. These details, if ever found out, are not top priority.

Situations like the one just described are also common for teachers of record. Instead of waiting until months have passed to *maybe* discover a child's needs, there should be a systematic way to understand home lives and then fill the gaps as needed. Imagine what a pre-planned, inclusive, classroom data set of basic human needs could change for a school learning community. Systematically seeking to understand another's basic needs can inform, plan, and support. This can be life changing in the classroom and in society.

Lately, there is a trend to recognize a child's social emotional learning needs at school. Some schools are hosting sessions that talk about social emotional well-being with the children. The children are given tips on how to self-regulate. While incorporating this seems like an advance, we must remember that students need more than just a lesson. Students need to learn

Table 1.1. Holt 1.0 Checklist of Basic Human Needs

Student Name:	Date:	Grade:	Assessed by:

This checklist is to help understand and support student's basic human needs. The goal is to identify the needs of your students, who are a part of the classroom community, by seeking to know more. This tool can help by identifying needs and then prompting needed conversations with student support services who can provide help as needed.

Note: This assessment should be used to help identify needs and conversate with other professionals helping provide resources. This should not be used for harm. When applicable, this assessment can be used to help inform discussions like/as Response to Intervention or other school-based learning community meetings. This is only an initial checklist.

Directions: Say to the person you are assessing: *"I am very glad I get the opportunity to work with you. It is important to me that each person in our classroom community have their basic needs met. Having our basic needs met helps us be more successful in all we do. If at any time you are uncomfortable, please know you do not have to answer my questions. Just know that the goal of this assessment is to connect with each member of our classroom community and help with any support that might be possible."*

Take notes in the "note column" and ask follow-up questions as needed.

Basic Need	Questions to Ask	Notes
Food	Do you feel like you have enough food to eat? What is your favorite food? What (if any) foods do you dislike?	
Clothing	Do you have clothes to wear?	
Personal/ Self-Care	Do you have personal self-care support? Examples might be: a place to shower if desired, an opportunity to wash your clothes, and access to other supplies to help you with personal self-care?	
Shelter	Do you have a place to live when you are not at school? If you do, what is this place like?	
Rest	Do you have a place to rest? If you do, what is this place like?	
Love	Do you feel loved by others?	
Happiness	Do you think of yourself as a happy person? If so, what makes you happy?	
Health	Do you feel healthy? Are there any health-related issues you want to tell me about?	
Belonging	Do you feel like you belong in your at-home family? Who makes up your at-home family? Do you feel like you belong with your classroom/school family?	
Subject/ Content	Thinking about your knowledge: What topics/subjects do you know a lot about? What (if anything) would you like to learn more about? What topics/subjects (if any) are more challenging for you?	
Other	Are there any other needs you want to tell me about?	

strategies for real-life situations that are happening in real time. We cannot assume that if we teach a lesson on social emotional needs, that during moments of crisis, a student will fluidly use the strategies that were shared with them.

Having a systematic community-centered school resource pipeline complete with a process to address identified needs should be in place. Early identification and support can help meet the needs of children. Early understandings can possibly make a way for early interventions and maybe avoid tragedies like the one in Parkland and Uvalde. Consider the benefits of this checklist of basic human needs.

Our schools and societies need an organized process to collect information and organize support to meet each student's basic needs. This can promote classroom success in the present and beyond. Schools must address needs of society. This includes the basic human needs of children they serve.

We must pause and investigate today's classrooms filling in the gaps of student's basic needs. We must realize that making sure basic human needs in a school system are met should also include the needs of others.

In addition to the basic needs of students, teachers who are leading students need their basic needs met as well. With the biggest teacher shortage in history, there is an overwhelming tone that teachers are fed up with being mistreated. There is more about the teacher shortage in chapter 5.

Teachers have credentials. For teacher certification, there are so many details required for the program and monitored through the accreditation process. Years of classes in both pedagogy and content, standardized exams, portfolios, logged time spent in the classroom, and documented observations must be mastered. Despite all the hard work, teachers do not feel respected.

Teachers deserve respect from society. Understanding and supporting should be the norm; not the afterthought when so many teachers have left the profession.

Actions are speaking for teacher value. Teacher pay and respect is low. Post–COVID-19, teachers are still struggling. Chapter 6 shares about the future teachers. For someone to pour into another, they must be filled. We know that teachers give so much, so what about their needs? Do we even ask or check in?

Teachers face a double whammy of burden. There is a lack of basic needs being met for their students and in some cases for themselves. Just like children, we must question if teachers leading the future, can be their best if they are not supported. As supporters, we should question leadership dispositions, policies, and service-related opportunities that impact teachers and then directly impact the students that schools are supposed to serve.

Dewey said that it is the community's moral duty to educate. He knew that it is the community's duty to organize and shape in ways that will move

Table 1.2. Questioning the Purpose of Schools

Students	Teachers	Communities' Role
Do we see students as leaders who identify needs and help make decisions and solve problems?	Do we see teachers facilitate leadership skills and truly allow students to be leaders?	
Do we see teachers and administrations acting like a dictator or facilitator of thinkers?	Do students have thinking skills that are higher level and see the deeper purposes of their schooling?	
Do teachers use outdated teaching styles (either on their own or suggested by the administration) that are a concern?	Are students responding to the methods of teaching with an engaged, purpose-seeking, growth-mindset?	
Do teachers feel heard and supported?	Do students feel heard and supported?	
Are school policies (official and unofficial) fair to teachers?	Are school policies (official and unofficial) fair to students?	
Do the policies and procedures the teachers must follow align with the world we want to live in?	Do the policies and procedures the students must follow align with the world we want to live in?	
Do teachers help establish student classroom jobs that are meaningful to the larger classroom and school community?	Do students see the connection between their classroom jobs and their own school community?	
Do teachers lead students to have a service-mindset?	Are frequent appropriate opportunities given to students to serve others in their community?	

society in the right direction. Dewey also knew that democratic leadership is essential for a democratic society. Consider the questions on the chart below. For each item, think about the purpose of school and why these may be lacking. What is the community's role in supporting students and teachers?

Members of society must be challenged to ask a teacher if they feel supported, respected, and valued. Ask political leaders if they make it a priority to visit with educators and other school leaders more often than they do with the lobbyists. Ask educators and school leaders if they are approached by political leaders and feel their concerns are heard. Sadly, often the majority of teachers are not respected.

One purpose of school should be to retain teachers. Thinking about the teacher shortage there is a correlation of mandated scripted curriculum, harsh teacher evaluations, and the copious amounts of stress and teacher burnout.

Teachers are aware that mandated curriculum consumes so much of public dollars, yet teacher raises rarely happen. Compare salaries among other professionals. Compare teacher bathroom break opportunities and the time they are given to consume their lunch against the lunch schedules of other professionals.

Teachers are expected to give up their basic human rights without hardly a notice from administration or citizens outside of the profession. Teachers do not get sufficient opportunities to use the restroom during the school day. This is because their classrooms are full of students who must always be supervised. There are articles written by experts, directed at teachers about their concerns for their bladder health. Teachers are known to drink less water, so they will not have to use the bathroom as much. Some report having frequent bladder infections. Before school, sometimes at lunch, and after school are the three main times teachers take bathroom breaks.

Teachers are often cut short on lunch breaks. During COVID-19, student lunchtime was moved from the cafeteria to the classrooms to avoid excessive interactions within the large group settings where the virus could spread. The solution was switching to sack lunches prepared in the cafeteria and delivered to the classrooms to eat. Teachers were now expected to give up their lunch breaks to sit with their class. Then teachers had to sanitize the learning space afterwards. More often than you know, this model is still happening in some settings today.

The models set for bathroom and lunch for teachers also impacts the model applied to students. Much like teachers, students, who need to learn social skills and self-care, experience limited bathroom time. Most times, these breaks are frowned upon.

Student lunch time is an average 15 minutes without any talking or social interactions allowed. Imagine if at-home bathroom opportunities and mealtimes were managed like school.

Many prospective teachers are being told to choose another profession altogether. Young students want to avoid school. When school environments are harsh, combined with a home life that is harsh, it is easy to see why students and teachers feel overwhelmed and defeated. When students and teachers are defeated, we should ask what is even the purpose of it all? It is true that when teachers themselves are not treated as professional members of their larger society, the students they serve suffer. There is a breakdown of the entire school system. This includes the tiniest of school communities that are needed.

Schools and Democracy

Dewey believed that democracy is deeper and broader than just a special type of government model. Dewey shared that democracy is a collective group of citizens that have faith in the continuous renewal of society. Democracy is believing collectively in the capacities of human nature. Dewey knew that having knowledge of the social conditions of present day needs for our civilization is a big part of understanding and building upon a child's powers. This building upon a child's powers is the democratic way.

In a democracy, the people should have a voice and help make decisions. This requires leaders that lead in ways that allow others to be heard. Also, the members of the democratic society must be willing to speak up and act when needed. When common needs are discovered and changes need to be made, everyone must play a part and make sure progression happens.

Dewey made a bold statement and said schooling can be a waste if teachers are not called upon to communicate. Schools are a place for teachers to have a voice about needed changes with policy. Dewey knew the importance of schools having shared responsibility between educators and society to bring about a true call to action. Knowing that schools need to function like a democracy, we must make sure that students and teachers have a voice.

Another part of democracy is the shared work responsibility we all have. We all have jobs that work together and play a part in our larger community. These jobs include, but are not limited to, public service, transportation, hospitality, and health care. Students, just like adults, benefit from school jobs that better the classroom and greater school community. These jobs can be as simple as a door greeter, student council member, technology team, or a food backpack delivery helper.

As shared above, there are simple ways that a democratic environment can be created in a classroom. The simple task of giving students jobs can improve the needed basic life skills like sweeping and learning to cook. Parents and the community should be included when possible. Students need life skills that will transfer into adulthood and support democracy. The established school systems should be a support.

As mentioned, building a community is very important. The community must maintain a strong relationship with parents. School systems have a variety of ways that parent connections are handled. Small meetings, parent-teacher conferences, and volunteer opportunities are just a few. Schools are to support and connect.

One meeting for parents commonly used by schools is the open house gathering. This meeting is a time that schools share basic information regarding things like school day pick-up, drop-off, basic behavior rules, and give the required Title II report. While these things are important, we should consider if the structure of the open house type of events is effectively building connections with parents and families. Schools should be inviting for parents and their ideas.

Dewey knew the importance of addressing life skills in school settings. Connections with parents (and families) in other ways like family cooking nights may be more impactful. Instead of an hour of talking at parents, including family cooking activities is a great way to incorporate reading, math, family, and life skills. There are more needs of families that schools should help with, and it is important to better understand what needs exist. Then parent night can be more than just talking and a real benefit to all involved.

The daily happenings at schools should be democratic. Currently, there are some common school practices that have continued to destroy democratic foundations. Students need to be treated fair just like we want as adults. By treating students unfairly, the sense of community can be destroyed. Common school practices should be examined and reworked as needed. Schools are meant to make sense.

Schools must make decisions about how to deal with issues like attendance and discipline. Looking at current school attendance policies and discipline practices, we find that these actions are often different than what we desire for a democracy. Schools are quick to act in undemocratic ways and give little thought about the damage their decisions may cause. If we want schools to match the best democratic societies, attendance norms and discipline policies should be revisited.

There is no simple way to deal with behavior issues. Often the situation that students are forced to deal with is the cause of the behavior. If a student appears to be a behavior problem, the first action that schools take is always some sort of isolation from the group. The isolation may be losing recess with peers, sitting alone in detention, suspension, or even expulsion if deemed necessary. Each of the school choices regarding which method of discipline is used for each unique situation has its own set of repercussions.

With suspension, the student is not allowed to attend school for a set time. The student is essentially banished from the school community and sometimes sent back into a home life that has struggles. Once an elementary student was suspended from school for three days over a playground fight. On a quick lunch run, the student was seen walking the streets all alone. While there may be serious reasons for suspension that must be taken into consideration, there are many situations where students are suspended for a very small thing. Either way, when an underage student is sent home and not allowed in the school, who is legally responsible for that child during the day? What if the child was left home alone due to a school suspension because parents were working? There are cases that suspended students have been left alone, injured, and in some cases even killed.

School policies should be looked at carefully and discussed ensuring the best moral and ethical practices are in place. School policies must also consider the need to help students become part of the community. If the purpose of the school is to be a place to learn social skills and practice ways to thrive in the community, the students who are having the most difficult time are often those who require extra help. Support cannot be given when the child is constantly removed from school.

SUMMARY CHALLENGE

The focus of this chapter reviewed the purpose of school. Dewey shared that schools are more than just a place to learn subject-specific content knowledge. Schools must become a place to develop social skills. To explore the needs of schools more deeply, we need to rethink our purpose of school and what we do each day to meet the goals we desire.

School must be a place that the child's basic needs are systematically monitored and addressed. The checklist shared in this chapter is a great resource for schools to implement. Reflecting on what Dewey said, it is easy to say "yeah, we do all that stuff" but the reality is that this is not the exact truth. A systematic thought process to understand and then act on behalf of a person's basic needs must be a priority. Teachers should also be remembered. Filling gaps will be an opportunity for communities to be involved and community-centered schools to form.

Dewey believed that schools and societies are one thing and should function as a democracy if we expect to maintain a democratic future. Dewey knew that if democracy is not tended to, it will quickly die. Our schools and the communities must be seen as one force making the world a better place.

Seeing the purpose of school in a new light is important. We must compare what we do in school that contradicts what we believe in. This will give us room to identify big needs and make changes. All members of the school, including teachers, should be treated as active members of change with a valued voice and respected classroom leader. Together we need to determine what the purpose of schools *should* be like, versus what they are.

This chapter shares the same themes as other chapters. We must remember that framing all things educational must be done with the purpose of school in mind.

Summary Questions:

1. Are children given opportunities to function in a school that mimics the real world?

2. Are today's schools full of mini-classroom democracies that replicate the desired society wanted in the outside world? Or are schools just the opposite? Why do you think thisis so?
3. Are children kind to one another? What part of kindness skills do the schools and communities actively work on? Why or why not? Are school's unfair policies a part of the problem?
4. What are the top reasons schools do not function as a democracy?
5. What specific steps that lead to change should begin to remove undemocratic policies and procedures and result in better schools and a better future?

Chapter Two

Children at the Center

"The child is the starting-point, the center, and the end."

—John Dewey

OVERVIEW

Dewey shared the need for schools to have a child-centered focus. He explained that having a child-centered focus should be the continuous driving factor in *all* educational decisions being made.

In response to Dewey's claim, most educators would agree that we all should have a child-centered focus. Many say that we already *have* a child-centered focus. However, when taking a closer look, a true child-centered focus is not what is happening in most schools.

If children are not the center of the school's focus, then we need to figure out what the focus is really about. Collectively, we must figure out what each school's focus is on. If not the child, we must seek to understand any unsuitable demands being placed on children. Unsuitable demands are resulting in an explosion of unwanted outcomes.

We need to identify who or what is the root cause for continuing to repeat decisions that negatively impact children. We can no longer remain complacent year after year. Schools that lack a child-centered focus need immediate change.

This chapter builds on the established idea that a child-centered focus is needed for all schools. There are five topics outlined in this chapter that help remind the world what it is a child really needs. We can then compare the child's needs to what we see happening in schools.

These five topics identify the child's needs:

- basic needs
- support with child development
- support with learning needs
- character development

We must keep in mind that to reach the goal of having a child-centered focus around a child's basic needs cannot be complete without analyzing the way the basic needs are being delivered. The school day structure and the communities' support impact the child's needs. Any disconnects in the school day structure that are identified should challenge us. We will need to begin to plan all decisions with a child-centered focus for the sake of our children and our future.

Children's Basic Needs

To be child-centered, we must remind ourselves what it is that a child needs to be whole. Whole Child research tells us that developing humans need to be healthy, supported, safe, challenged, and engaged for the best chance of success. Maslow's Hierarchy of Basic Needs have similar identified components. Maslow's Hierarchy of Needs tells us that a child's physical well-being, safety, love, belonging, esteem, and self-actualization (the desire to belong) must be met throughout their development.

It is critical to recognize that these basic needs overlap. While examining one area of need, other areas of need are connected. For example, the need for a child to feel safe is connected to having a place to shelter and enough food to eat. The need for belonging is connected to the need to feel loved. Today's school systems and the collective community are not focusing on how to fulfill most of the basic needs. Without a child's needs being met, expecting a child can develop a plethora of subject-specific content knowledge is illogical.

Good teachers understand that a child's basic needs are important to classroom success. A friend shared a video created and posted online by a teacher. In the video, the teacher shared the care closet she created for her classroom. Her care closet was fully stocked with food, clothes, and personal hygiene items. She had created this care closet so her students could have access to a few of the basic items needed.

Teachers should not face the task of meeting all student's basic needs alone. As a community, systematic collaboration with teachers regarding students' needs and working together to find a solution keeps children's needs at the center. Using a systematic checklist like the *Holt 1.0 Checklist of Basic*

Human Needs shared in chapter 1 would be a beneficial tool to know what basic needs the students have and inform what might be added to the care closet and with other similar services.

In the video, the care closet was stocked with food. When thinking about a child's basic needs, ensuring they have enough food to eat is an important place to begin. Without food, the task of learning is made more difficult and sometimes impossible. When hungry, the human brain will shift its focus on the need to obtain food. Food is needed for survival and the need for survival will take over.

When hungry, thoughts of food trump other given tasks like mastering subject-specific school content. Mastering algebraic equations are not a priority in a child's life when their basic food needs are not met. Some of the hardest teacher tasks are having to deal with the pressures to guarantee that a child advances through subject-specific content knowledge even when the child is starving.

Pivotal, life-changing moments take place during the first years of a person's teaching journey. One pivotal moment was in my fourth-grade classroom during our daily block of class writing time. The class was given the prompt "write a story detailing what the best day ever would be." This writing prompt was selected because it is basic enough that any child would have an easy time coming up with ideas to demonstrate their writing abilities. Knowing that a few students might need extra support getting started, a small kidney-shaped table area was set up to work one-on-one with anyone needing extra help.

A young boy caught my eye when scanning the class. He was reluctant to complete his writing assignment. To be honest, this boy *refused* to write. To help give him more support, he was moved from his desk to the kidney-shaped table. Moving meant he would be closer in teacher proximity making it easier to give direct scaffolding support.

What happened next was a full-on power struggle. Classroom teachers know that power struggles with students can be difficult to navigate. This is especially true when the rest of the class has looked up from their work and are watching the power struggle event unfold. All the students knew that the writing assignment directions had been given to them orally and were written on the board. The writing assignment was expected to be complete, and the directions were to be followed with no exceptions.

The battle began to *make* this child write his story and tell about his best day ever. Forty-five minutes later . . . after a long, intense power struggle, full of back and forth give and take, teacher victory was achieved! The young boy finally had a completed a three-paragraph essay.

As a novice teacher, this feat felt very accomplished. Reflecting on the situation, this event seemed like a moment of strength and because of this accomplishment, the classroom order was saved! The well-managed classroom order would be rewarded by the principal.

Later on that afternoon was the daily teacher preparation period. During this time, the children visited the art room for their weekly art class session. This hour was quiet time for teachers to spend planning, answering emails, and grading student work.

Setting with the stack of writing prompts, the task to grade the boy's work began. What was realized with the boy's work was hard to believe. Even though he had been given direct help, it was the overall analysis of his work that was a surprise. The final words the boy had written caused my new teacher heart to sink. His story was something unforgettable. It started out something like this:

My Best Day Ever

My best day ever would be spent with my Poppa. We would start off by gathering our fishing poles and walking to the lake. It would be fun, and I would be happy.

Next, was an entire page (top to bottom) filled with this kind of content:

We would catch the fish and cook it. We would eat it. Yum Yum! Then we would go to McDonalds and get a juicy cheeseburger. I would eat it all up. After that we would go hunting for a deer. We would fry up the deer meat and eat it. Last, we would stop by Burger King and get fries and ice cream. . . . I would be very full and fat.

My mind began to race trying to connect all sorts of recent facts about this student. This child was tall and very skinny. His pants were worn in the knees and a little too short in the ankles. Earlier in the month, the cafeteria worker had been fussing to me about him taking extra grain bars at breakfast. The realization that this kid was *starving* finally clicked!

The conclusion of the event left a feeling that this teacher was the worse person in the world for demanding this child write when he was so hungry. He was having a hard time, and his closest school support had no clue what was being asked of him. The most important focus was getting the completion of his writing assessment. Grades must be complete for the report card or face trouble from the principal. The child's food insecurities never crossed my mind as even a possibility. Focusing on a child's basic needs must be at the center of all we do.

Dewey shared that as a preservice teacher or for someone who has just become a teacher, the true learning has only begun. Novice educators are just learning what it takes for classroom success. Teachers, young and old, must understand that it takes a willingness to be a life-long learner and an unwavering commitment to understand students' needs to thrive. Understanding the importance of basic needs and the impact these basic needs have on a teacher's pedagogy, teaching subject-specific content knowledge, and the larger society must be a continuous thread woven into life.

Unfortunately, cases like the boy and his writing assignment are far too common. As shared in chapter 1, school meals are not free. Extra long weekends and extended holidays are scary for so many kids who lack a home with available food.

Many believe, that as an educator, it's not their job to worry about food insecurities. The time it takes to identify and seek solutions for food insecurities is certainly not planned for in the teacher's workday schedule. The expectation is that teachers remain focused on the subject-specific content knowledge goals that are being closely monitored.

The takeaway from this is that what is in the best interest for the child was and continues to not be a pressing goal of the school day. To keep children at the center, basic needs, like dealing with child hunger, should be planned for. We need to rethink the structure of the day, the expectations placed upon teachers, and that we are making sure that the basic needs are met.

Continuing with the topic of having children at the center of all we do and discussing the basic need for food, there is another side that we must analyze. In the realm of education, there is this common practice of using food as a reward. Often this reward is used when students can demonstrate certain subject-specific content knowledge that is connected to goals.

Teachers, on their own or as part of an accepted school culture, often use food as a reward. Candy, popcorn parties, pizza celebrations, and trips to get a Happy Meal are used to reward students who meet certain academic milestones.

There is an incredible amount of discussion that can be had about this common practice with food and doing what is best for children. Many would report that the practice of using food as a reward is not intended to be harmful. However, when looking deeper, we need to consider what we are really doing to the mind of a child when we use food to reward academics.

We must question if we believe that food should be a reward exchanged for intelligence with developing children. Has there been consideration given to students with a learning disability and how they might be disadvantaged and not receive as many food rewards as their peers? Do children who are diabetic or those with food allergies feel they are less smart than their peers? What about children who struggle with obesity?

Related to food, there are flashbacks of memories from the time that a student walking down the hallway nearly choked on a hard candy she had been given for a snack. The candy lodged in her throat. The child's life was saved when another teacher quickly stepped in and performed the Heimlich maneuver. This life-changing moment will forever haunt me.

Fresh fruits and vegetables make great snacks for most students if access is possible. However, using food of any kind as a reward for academics (or behavior) needs more thought. The basic need for food impacts all other needs and using food as a motivator should be discussed.

In summary, when it comes to the basic need for food to eat, we know food matters and that we should make sure that children have enough food. However, if we expect children to meet rigorous academic school goals, the way the school system functions and specifically addresses food insecurities along with the other basic needs should be considered *first* before demanding academic success.

Children need the chance to attend a school where they can participate in a democratic system as they develop into adults. Children should attend a school where they can grow and develop while learning developmentally appropriate content knowledge. Without this, the child can struggle with belonging, moral reasoning, and ethical sense making.

The developing child needs to attend school. School attendance is important. Studies have proven there is a correlation between attendance and school success. Therefore, the constant monitoring of attendance is another big part of the school culture.

In some cases, schools use attendance as a reward. This might seem sensible and encouraging for some. Before we use attendance as a reward, we must recognize that the task of getting to school can be a school requirement that students worry about. For some students, the overwhelming steps it takes to get to school can impact their mental health. Students are often penalized for attendance issues that are out of their control. Many of the students facing issues out of their control can be damaging.

For example, students sometimes miss catching their school bus because they must wake themselves for school. Many students must wake themselves plus get a younger sibling ready for school. Together they must be at the bus stop on time. Many children do not have a parent at home until they catch the bus or a parent with access to a car that has enough gas to drive them to school.

Some children have parents that check them out early from school. If a parent chooses to check their child out of school early, the child is not in control of their attendance. When thinking about students who face chronic health issues and extended illnesses that cause hospital stays, attendance rules tied to rewards can be even more discouraging.

A general rule is that if choosing to implement a reward system for anything child related, it is important that the system is designed in a way that children can *earn* rewards for things that are *in their control*. Otherwise, we can have the opposite impact. Instead of encouraging school, school can be a place of discouragement. These negative feelings create a school culture that leaves students feeling defeated, confused, and disjointed due to unfair or inappropriate actions put in place at the school. When this happens, coming to school may become a stressful time and cause a lack of connection.

A school that is satisfied with students who are outcasted, disconnected, and discouraged may see a decline in attendance and a rise in gang-related activity. Students need to belong, and if they do not feel a sense of belonging, they will find a place to belong with negative groups of people who make them feel included.

There are various viewpoints about what school behavior should look like and how this is connected to the child's basic needs. Regarding school behavior expectations, as a united society, we need to first remember the basic needs of a child. Specifically that the students need to be a part of a democratic system that is fair and just starting at a very young age.

We must be honest with the flaws within our established school structures and systems that have become engrained in our belief system over time. Unfair or unjust school structures and systems will set a child back both academically and socially the minute trouble arises.

We must teach and grow children instead of separating them from opportunities to learn and become better. Schools today systematically set students up for failure because of unfair expectations. Students are placed in classroom environments that are inappropriate and unable to meet their needs.

The school's idea of what constitutes good behavior and how to respond to "bad" behavior is damaging. There is an accepted model about learning, behavior, and discipline that has developed from an inaccurate idea. This model says that learning and good behavior looks like groups of children who sit in stillness and silence, stay in neat rows for extended periods of time, and happily soak up subject-specific content knowledge. Society has accepted this model of what good behavior and authentic learning looks like and we discipline anything that looks different.

The decisions being made regarding what is appropriate with discipline-related protocols and procedures are misaligned to the most basic child needs. Schools have decided that certain unnatural behaviors should be seen as the correct behaviors. School systems that unfairly judge "when and what" disciplinary actions are to be in place negatively impact a student's education, esteem, and belonging.

All things discipline-related are very complicated. Because of this, many feel that schools are against parents and students are against the school. For the betterment of children and society, restructuring our belief system related to learning, classroom behaviors, and discipline practices must find a common ground that centers around the child. Starting with intrinsic motivation is the key.

For both immediate and long-term success, students need to be intrinsically motivated. Students should be conditioned to think about their own learning needs and the important role they have as a member of their society. This helps students to be self-driven. Dewey shared that when teachers and other school officials are frustrated with student behavior and/or academic performance, often tactics are used that cause the opposite of intrinsic motivation to unfold. These tactics are not good for children.

Some of the tactics used in the classroom cause harm and Dewey cautioned us about using them many years ago. Dewey knew that these certain types of tactics schools use were short lived, if they worked at all, and he felt that the negative implications on children should be weighed against the desire to persuade them and get the immediate results we think are important.

Some educators rely on using perpetuating fears of retention to make students work harder and perform a certain way. To pass their current grade and be promoted to the next level, certain things must be accomplished.

Once a principal explained that she never heard anyone as an adult say how glad they were to have been held back in a grade. She explained she would never retain another student because of the many hardships that resulted from it. Retention is another very common practice that should be discussed and weighed heavily before deciding to use.

When students are retained in a grade, it is not forgotten. Children make friends with classmates and then see their friends move ahead. They are held back with students who are now younger in age. Since their new classmates are not their age, students must face developmental milestones alone. Things like puberty can be hard to manage when all the others around you are not experiencing the same changes. This feeling can cause isolation.

Sometimes students are retained in lower grades and then a few years later it is discovered that they have a learning disability. How discouraging to be confronted as a child about low performance, be unable to keep up with the expectations, and then be retained, only to find out you have an issue with cognitive processing or dyslexia.

Another common tactic that is harmful and used frequently is threatening students that they will be staying late or left behind from their peers if certain things are not accomplished. Staying after school, being placed in Saturday school, summer school, or missing other social time to sit in detention can cause a negative connection to schoolwork and the teachers. This is especially true when students are facing issues that are out of their control. To a child, it can seem they are being punished for trying to survive their life as best they can.

Other ways of unhealthy motivation can be when the fear of not making money and getting a future job is continuously used to get a student to accomplish certain academic tasks. This can cause feelings of confusion about their position in society. Using any type of fears or bribes such as using incentives like an extra movie day, recess, or a popcorn party for a certain school performance does not build an intrinsic desire to learn and grow. It can turn students away from school.

Last, the tactic of bargaining for the teacher's affection can be harmful. Parents can make this worse by saying things like "Mr. Smith is going to be so upset that you didn't do good on your test" or "I bet the principal knows you didn't finish your assignment." This type of tactic can put teachers, parents, and principals on one side against students who feel alone.

Some twenty years ago when visiting a Bahamian country, there was a newspaper article written to the public. It was specifically directed to parents and teachers. This article gave graphic details and images of children who had been beaten at school. The article was an effort to spread awareness that the common practice of beating a child was not helping children want to come to school. It went on to say that these beatings were believed to be the reason the children were running away.

Today in many school settings across the globe, paddling in a variety of forms is still used. Paddling is controversial for many, but regardless, we can understand that being hit with a board or other object can make a child hesitant to attend and become afraid of school.

Some readers might remember being hit in some way as a punishment in school. Some may specifically remember being hit with a ruler on the back of the hand when being scolded. Dewey knew that the old rapping of the knuckles with a ruler to gain attention would cause an association of fear and attending school in children. Listening to previous generations tell stories about being hit or watching a classmate being hit by a teacher is scary for children and even grown adults. While some students may have seemed to act differently after being threatened or hit, it's hard to imagine that this tactic improves long-term knowledge over time and makes students love school more.

Dewey shared that some children may shut down and give up, while others may seem to be more involved and decide to be an active learner. We must know that some of the active student participants are really not interested and see school as a series of tasks within their daily routine that they just need to get through to survive.

As Dewey shared, we must realize that any new appeals or tactics used in school, whether they be positive or negative, will not last forever. Only through a child's own true interest in life and learning will we achieve the results we want for immediate tasks that carry over into long periods of time.

Unfortunately, the negative types of motivation mentioned are common practices used in schools. Television and movies continue to pass along a wrong version of what school should be like. This makes it even harder to change inaccurate beliefs in society.

Where do parents and community fit into the shaping of schools? Recently, during a back-to-school night, colorful, virtual slides were shared to inform parents and students about the expectations for the upcoming school year. As usual, there were some slides dedicated to the car rider line pickup and drop-off procedures and steps to pay for lunch fees. But overwhelmingly, the theme of the slides was incredibly negative. This heavy, dark, back-to-school kick off caused a sick feeling in the tummies of so many children and parents.

One big rule shared on the slides was that no technology was allowed at school. No technology being allowed is a common rule in place in many schools. At this back-to-school event, the no-technology rule seemed comical since the slides being shared to students and parents by the school were virtual. It was encouraged that the slides be accessed using your smart phone to scan the given QR code. Being virtual allowed the slides to be seen more easily and reassessed later on.

Furthermore, this rule is interesting since technology is a tool that is very much needed in life. Parents use technology. Teachers and administrators use technology. Future jobs require technology experience, but the thought of students using technology at school like they do everywhere else is a big NO. Write ups and disciplinary actions would be serious for this offense. This rule is an example of convenience and learning real life-skills over authoritative control.

Continuing with technology rules, uncharged laptop devices were a big NO. All school-required laptops must be charged each night at home and brought back each day. It was explained that this charging expectation is a big one for classrooms to function. What about charging stations at schools? We have charging stations at hospitals, restaurants, in our cars, and even in the arms of our couches!

If absent, it was shared that students were to log into their Google classrooms and explore. Looking around in the virtual space was how students would be able to locate and complete all work from the day of school they missed. For upper grades, six Google classrooms were each set up differently. This seemed extremely overwhelming if a child was ever to be sick. It seemed there would be no time for reteaching skills and all information needed was found in virtual classroom shells.

To summarize, there is a common rule that no technology can be used during school except the ones the schools decide are okay. The technology the school provides better come back to school each day fully charged. Other, similar, and familiar, devices must be off and unseen, or a disciplinary action would result. What if the idea of using the proper technology to learn was given? Do these rules and disciplinary actions make sense? Are we supporting children or actually setting them up for failure?

As an educational team, it is important to dissect all small and big school details looking out for the best interests of children. Decisions about a child's physical well-being, safety, love, belonging, esteem, and self-actualization (the desire to belong) must be considered. Let's focus on gaining students' interest and not making them afraid.

Child Development

The natural development of children must be considered. There are stages and milestones that students are transitioning through. Dewey said that it is when we recognize there are urgencies for child development that must be acted upon in their own way, that we can begin to have a firm basis that all other things can build upon.

Dewey believed that we violate a child's natural development when we expect children to master special studies like writing or geography outside of their normal social life. In addition to Dewey, there are other experts who are noted today for their work regarding the human development and the process of learning. John Locke was a 17th-century philosopher who argued that the mind is a blank slate and that it is filled up as humans experience life. Paulo Freire knew that critical thinking is positive for growth and that education is never neutral. Lev Vygotsky argued that cognitive abilities are socially guided, and he created the concept of the zone of proximal development centering on children and the way learning develops.

By the time children begin school at five years old, their mind and experiences have already begun to develop. For a child, making it through life, as it exists, is so complex according to Dewey. Therefore, adults should carefully consider the extra pressures put on students.

All the pieces of the human puzzle are factors that are made from what a person understands and how each unique learner synthesizes new experiences. Avoiding unneeded and excessive pressures for students includes the excessive stress with the way the school functions. A student's required participation in school should not make daily life so much harder.

In addition to schoolwork requirements, some children are faced with harsh realities. Some come from families that believe children should be seen but not heard. Abuse, neglect, and food insecurities are just a few of the extra challenges some children face. When school adds additional pressure, this can lead to a dangerous situation.

A child needs movement to learn. Movement helps with mental growth. Yet hour by hour during the school day, movement is restricted and, in some cases, disciplined. Dewey cautioned that when teachers feel pressured and can't seem to get students to focus, teachers blame the students (or the human) instead of what kind of inappropriate treatment we are putting them through.

Dewey spoke about how a child's restless activities may seem senseless to adults. He believed this is because adults don't learn that way anymore. We should not expect a young person to sit for long periods of time without movement. Children learn by moving.

Children should be motivated to learn. Often as adults, we think that just lecturing a child by saying that what they learn in school is important or using scare tactics and discipline will do the trick. Dewey gave an adult example of motivation for us to ponder. His example was about a husband who has a wife and a family. Before getting married, the husband was unmotivated to work. After he marries and has a family, he now has a motive for his daily work expectations. His post-marriage motive to work is not because he is more interested in the work than he was before he was married. It's that the husband knows that the task to work is now a hardship that he can't escape from to support his family. Children are similar in that they might do the task if there is no escape, but it is likely that they have no real care about it.

The adult example is important because children are not living the same life timeline as the husband in the example. Authentic engagement with children needs a highly qualified educator who creates learning obstacles that can inspire the learner to stop and think. Dewey continued to explain that a good teacher, who knows the child and understands that introducing the appropriate kind of engaging obstacles, is a positive thing. A teacher can help the child embrace difficulties, connect the importance of learning to their life, all while monitoring and helping students stay on the right track.

In summary, the child's basic needs should be the foundation of education. The way that learning occurs throughout the developmental scope of a child's life must be understood and embraced by educational leaders. Teachers and administrators need dispositions that support the individual child's needs and incorporate proper guidance. Using the child's individual strengths, love languages, and life experiences is a necessity.

Learning Needs and Character Development

As discussed, there is a disconnect between a child's learning needs and what we see happening in today's classroom. There is an ongoing misalignment between what we know a child needs and what we expect a child can do each day.

This misalignment impacts a child's character development. Dewey shared that a person's character is something that is formed and not taught. He also explained that we are all a part of the process it takes to guide one's developing character, and the child needs to be at the center.

Dewey shared that it is impossible to know what the future will be like twenty years from now. Dewey knew that instead of trying to plan and drill for something we can't predict, our time with children should be focused on giving the child command of their self. If a child has command of their self and understands the full use of their capacities, we can then prepare the child to face whatever tomorrow brings. When children are really at the center, the classroom experience we observe will be very different.

Character development and discipline are connected. While skimming through a Facebook parent group, there was a Reel that caught my eye. To help, here is a little background. Many school districts have a uniform policy and many strict sub-rules to go with it. Any change in these policies cause everyone to start the school year off in a panic. Parents are trying to understand the policy and any changes that have been made. Once the rules are understood, it will be possible to begin buying school clothes and supplies accordingly.

While there are strict rules about uniform pants and polo shirts, wearing a sweater-type jacket had previously been allowed. The policy states that there are no hoods allowed. Teachers had issues with headphone usage during school hours. Because of this, having a hood on a jacket was prohibited.

A new update to the sweater-type jacket policies was a big debate online. For the upcoming school year, the color of the sweater-type jacket was being enforced to only school colors. This requirement was said to be strictly enforced. While this might seem like a reasonable request that sweaters need to be school colors and hoods are banned, the truth is that purchasing a sweater with no hood, in specific colors, is quite difficult.

Rumors in the Facebook group were that children being caught in the wrong color or wearing a sweater with a hood would receive a discipline write-up. One post said that anyone wearing a sweater with a hood was getting it taken away from them the very first thing each morning.

The Reel was made by a student in high school facing the hoodie rules. In the Reel, there was a young student sitting in a classroom wearing a uniform. There was a voice dub-over of a pretend officer yelling to take laptops out of the bag and if wearing a hoodie to TAKE IT OFF! The caption referenced the school policy and insinuated that students were being treated like prisoners in a jail.

A variety of additional comments were left for readers to see regarding hats, backpacks, and electronic devices being taken. These comments were receiving "likes" from dozens of others. As shared, trying to find a solid, sweater-type jacket in a certain color, without a hood is not easy—especially for those who struggle financially.

This same type of situation regarding proper uniforms and disciplinary rules has consequences. For some, this means that students come to school wearing clothes that are too big, too small, or sometimes dirty. Students might come to school wearing wet clothes that didn't get dried the night before. Some students may get sent home instead of learning with their peers that day for not wearing the right clothes.

The pros and cons of enforcing a uniform policy is a big debate. However, if a decision is made to enact and enforce policies like this, we must consider the impact it has on the students and families.

- Is it true that we really see more benefits than downfalls when students are mandated to wear school uniforms?
- Should uniforms be provided for students and paid for in the school budget the same as desks and running water?
- Do uniforms make school feel like jail?
- Is this policy good for human development?
- Is punishment for clothing good for character development?
- Are there other ideas that might work better?

Dewey shared that learners need to play. This play includes dramatic learning opportunities to explore dolls (humanity), clothes (personal care), home (community), food (nutrition), and dishes (pottery). In school today, students might be given these topics to learn about, but often they are simulations of life at best. Most often, students are given thick workbooks they can barely hold to fill out.

Students need to learn to question. Dewey believed that open-ended questions and play opportunities must be given to children. Dewey gave an example for math and questioning: "How would you solve for x if you had to?" Students need to be encouraged to use their imagination instead of a worksheet where there is only one right way to solve problems. Students need to explore relevant data and spend time reflecting.

For character needs, Dewey shared that a reflective learner begins to understand the development of their own attitudes and dispositions. The habits and behaviors students form lead to their actions. We want the behaviors that students possess to result in better, self-regulated lives. This means we need to provide students with experiences that allow self-regulation to form.

The School Day

When thinking about having children at the center, we should think about where the children physically spend most of their time. Around the world, children spend most of their days in school.

- In America, children are in school each year from fall until early summer. This equals about 10 months in school out of the year.
- Australian students spend from late-January to mid-December in school with only a few weeks for summer break.
- In Japan, it is more like a year-round school. Students attend five days a week and some require Saturdays.

Many other countries such as France, Mexico, and Russia are all very similar. Across the world, children are in school almost year-round for an average of eight hours each day. The school day begins early in the morning and extends into the afternoon. Attendance is collected and documented for records. It is the law in America and in most other countries that children attend school each day.

Attendance expectations were not always like it is today. Currently the school day begins around 8 a.m. and ends around 3 p.m. From a global perspective, we can look at history and see that the school attendance expectations have fluctuated over time. School schedules have been a result of the needs that were best for an agrarian society. Now the school day schedule is centered around what is best for an industrialized society.

In the past, children worked on family farms for most of the day. School attendance was scheduled around the harvest needs. For decades, attending school up to the 6th grade was a big accomplishment. It wasn't until the early 1900s that students in America were required to finish school at least through elementary.

Despite the research that say early days and extended afternoons are not the best for children, the 8 a.m. to 3 p.m. school day is in place to align with the parent's industrialized work schedule. In an abundance of cases, parents are often on their jobs until 5 p.m. Most children are in after-school care until their parents are done for the day.

Since the progression of the industrial revolution, children were no longer needed to help with the family farm. Changing the school day schedule from 8 a.m. to 3 p.m. allowed parents to leave their children in care of the teacher while they tended to the shift demands of their jobs. We saw the hardships of schools being closed to the COVID-19 pandemic. No one was left to care for the children while their parents worked; this was especially difficult for the parents who were declared essential workers.

Since children are required to be in school from 6 years old until they are 18, we must look deeper into the decisions about what happens during the school day. We must watch what effect the school day requirements have on the development and behaviors of children.

We know that while children are developing, there are specific amounts of time that should be devoted to sleep. A lack of sleep has been connected to student frustrations with daily tasks, outbursts, and an increase in suicidal thoughts. We need to look at the amount of sleep time students need compared to the mandated school day schedule. We should not keep rules in place simply because they support the economic needs. What is best for the child should be important.

Requiring an early school day start time to allow parents to work in industrialized jobs for solid blocks of time during the day can be disadvantageous. We must remember that the desire to see the child grow and develop cannot center around the professional world. Growth means looking at the needs of the whole child. When the school day is set up in a way that violates the child's nature, we are not doing what is ethically right for the best interests of the child.

Children need time in their school day to rest. Some countries shut down mid-day to rest. There must be scheduled time built in to play, learn to tie their shoes, learn about life, and rest! Schools today are mostly subject-specific content focused. Dewey knew that prematurely requiring young children to master content-specific studies like geography or writing is not best practices for the child. Content studies should not dominate the child's life and their natural right to develop as a person.

Dewey explained that true education comes through the child's stimulation. The child's own interest and social situations they find themselves in are the basis of motivation. The school day set up needs revised to better meet the physical and social needs of the students it is meant to serve.

We must look at the school day for all the small practices that are misleading. When claiming to be doing what is best for the child, it is often not true. In several cases, we have major misconceptions about doing what is right for kids and changing what is wrong. We need to think about change and how we will rebuild the school systems after having lived generational inaccuracies.

The great majority of teachers and parents think that school is synonymous with discipline. As shared, many believe that children should sit in rows, appear to be listening to the teachers, and speak only when spoken to. If there is any talking and movement observed, it must mean that there is a bad teacher and running a class where nothing is learned. This idea has helped continue to shape the entire school day in a way that does not keep the child's needs at the center. Dewey insisted that the models of students sitting in rows, constantly regurgitating rote memorization of facts was old-fashioned and incorrect.

As mentioned, the need to move is important for a child's development, and we need more movement in the school day. *John Dewey challenged us to imagine if all the children were to sit and stare saying nothing at all.* What would be concluded about a child or children that had no movement? Do we really want children who sit completely still and don't speak? If not, then why do we continue to enforce harsh rules that deny talking and movement?

Deciding what kind and how much movement is appropriate for a child is not an easy task. This is because all learners have different needs. We need to uncover ways to get past the outdated mind-set that children are learning only when they are not talking and are only well-behaved when they are sitting silently in rows. Children do not learn like this, and we need to adjust the school models and combat misinformation.

Dewey encouraged teachers to see the necessity of movement with the development of children. He believed that movement of the eyes, lips, reading, and writing are all good forms of movement. Dewey went on to say that even if the movement being observed is something as simple as eye movement used in reading, we must remember that there is so much more movement in the child's spirit!

Dewey shared that if movement is discouraged, students might daydream and try to get themselves to a place where the movement they need can happen. Dewey shared that denied, unorganized movement leads to mischief, and we should not be surprised when it happens.

Regarding high school, Dewey spoke about the need for teachers to be leaders and help their class to recognize the importance of ethics, building relationships, and how their individual actions have an impact on the world. The school day should be careful not to suppress the bad times, because it will equally suppress the good.

Community and the Child

The well-being of the child and the health of our schools need the community to be involved. What happens inside the school matters, but Dewey shared that the community needs to think about the out-of-school needs children have. This kind of community involvement should be continuous and united. Decision makers need to be checked on and challenged when needed.

Decision makers are a big part of the child's life. Let's review the chain of decision makers. At the bottom of the chain, we have school administration. Most administrators involved in school leadership enforce decisions that are heavily influenced by policy. Many school administrators have little to do with the big decisions that are being made. Often they are left to enforce decisions they were not really consulted about. These decisions may have to do with dress code, classes they offer, the quality of the lunches, and the steps taken to resolve discipline issues. Several have expressed that they feel like they are more of an enforcer of rules than a cultivator of ideas. While the teachers are one level removed from administrators, they are very close in the decision enforcing level.

The school board is next. They are one level above administration. These members are the local policy makers. Their service is so important. The school board is often swamped with small things that take up a tremendous amount of time. Often, they are focused on budgets and monitoring the impact of the school budget within the community.

The school board decides on things like budgets, transportation, food service contracts, hiring and firing of employees, and student-focused policies. They also deal with a lot of angry people who are frustrated about things that the school board had little to do with.

Next, we have elected state-serving politicians. These decision makers are higher up the chain and are often unfamiliar with the needs of education and the play-by-play struggles. They may be experts in other fields like transportation or law. Mostly, these decision makers rely on a few loud voices and their own school-related experiences to make decisions about education.

At the top of the decision maker chain, there are business leaders. Influential businesses market and sell educational materials. They promise to fix all ideas. These businesses are making a huge profit off education and have found ways to be very influential with politicians.

Dewey warned that economically and politically controlling people can have great influence on educational decisions. If money or political power are the focus, manipulation by influential people with agendas, can take over school boards, policy makers, book publishers, and curriculum creators. Dewey warned that when this happens, children and parents will never be the center.

It is comforting to imagine that the politicians and school board members act in ways they feel are in the best interest of the child. While some higher up leaders may have the best intentions, there are many who do not care to get involved in the small details of education. Many are influenced by the loudest voices. Often the loudest voices are not coming from teachers in the classrooms.

There is a strange denial and avoidance of truth seeking when it comes to our educational issues. Our society haphazardly, if at all, is willing to take on the honest facts about school-related decisions and the problems that result. Seldom, outsiders are invested in understanding the ways decisions are being made and played out in the lives of teachers and students.

Many choose not to engage in debates about what we are doing in school and if it is best for children. There is an odd lack of fact checking. Maybe believing illusions that our school systems are doing right by children is easier than taking on the task to fix what is broken.

Parents must be a part of the community that supports the child. Today's parents fit into two categories. One group, the largest, see no urgent need to speak out. These parents expect their children to follow the rules. These parents are careful to speak out about things they find a bit odd. This complacency is often reflective of the way that they were raised.

The other category of parents may seem to be troublemakers that are overstepping. While these parents tend to be more vocal and may organize in groups, often they are at their wits ends and want fairness for their child. These groups may reach out to the administration and the school board with their dislikes. Often times, these parents get frustrated and many have filed lawsuits. Some give up and decide public school is not for their family.

Parents depend on schools to be organized, to hire qualified teachers, support teacher needs, and effectively monitor the development and social interaction of their children each day. Few parents question the big ideas that drive the school leadership's decisions and the reasoning behind the daily structure of school. Most parents rarely question whether their child's well-being is really the center of all things school-related. If it looks like their child is okay, there seems to be little to worry about.

Parents must trust the system because they themselves are so busy trying to survive the day. Parents have time-consuming tasks with their own careers. Some parents are attending college, dealing with health needs, or other non-negotiables that consume their time.

Parents (and other members of the community) have memories of their own past educational experiences. These memories are often loosely compared with the happenings in today's schools. Challenges faced like bullying, learning disabilities, poverty, and real-world preparedness seem to work themselves out. Overall, from the outside perspective things with school appear the same.

As grown-ups, who feel they survived similar schooling experiences, there is an underlying idea that all turned out okay with their old-school challenges, and it will be the same for this generation. Since the past generations turned out all right, many believe society should not be too alarmed with small issues.

SUMMARY CHALLENGE

The purpose of this chapter is to remind us that children should be the center of all we do that is school related. This idea brings out a slew of school practices that are not child centered. The examples shared in this chapter can help schools to reflect on a more personal level about their own policies and practices that may or may not be centered around the child.

Some examples to consider include meeting students' basic needs, avoiding fear-based motivation, building intrinsic motivation, and establishing connections to the school day tasks being asked of children. When looking at things in place in school compared to the child's needs (that align and support natural development) we can see room for improvement. We need a more child-centered focus that will improve content knowledge, character development, and more.

Putting the school day details under a microscope will allow a deep dive into our educational structures, policies, and procedures in place that may be harming the child and society. Looking for ways to support teachers as facilitators who will build a school world that puts the needs of students first and prepares for the future is best.

It is not enough to assume that students are the center of education. The community must ask and ensure this is happening, avoiding unfair political overreach. Together, let us think about what actions are lacking and what *should* happen to place children at the center and make change.

Summary Questions:

1. If children and teachers are not consulted about what is being done each day at school, then who is making the decisions? Is it lobbyists, policy makers, or for-profit curriculum companies?
2. Is there a systematic way that students' basic needs are being monitored and met? If not, how might this change? What supports are needed?
3. Are teachers supported in doing what is best for their students?
4. What unfair practices are in place that do not have the best interest of the child in mind? How can this be changed?
5. What specific steps can be put into action that will unite parents, students, and communities to continuously monitor the needs of the students and what is being done to address issues and advocate for change?

Chapter Three

How We Teach

"The subjects we teach must be an experience for our students."

—John Dewey

OVERVIEW

Pedagogy is the method and practice of teaching. In the medical world, it is often said the doctor treating a patient is "practicing" medicine. The term "practicing" medicine makes sense since the best medical treatment is a result of a research process. Medicine will forever be an ongoing learning experience. The continuous practice of medicine adapts preexisting methods to meet the needs of patients. As technology advances, the approach a medical doctor uses to provide the best possible treatment method to a patient could likely change if the new treatment is proven to be better.

Like medicine, teaching can also be thought of as a practice. As times change, the practice of teaching should be advancing and evolving to meet the needs of the society it serves. We must recognize that the needs of society have changed a great deal over the past decades. The ways we approach the practice of teaching should mirror that change.

Dewey said that for successful teaching, the child's life must be the focus. Educators cannot simply be expected to give lessons that will result in learning if the child's life is not considered. Dewey said that we must learn to see life as a child. We must learn to push aside adult experiences (or take out the "adult") to connect with children.

Teachers are tasked with helping to prepare students who graduate ready to go into the world and be self-sufficient. Students will need skills to work and be productive in their communities. As mentioned in chapter 1, so much has changed in the world and with the jobs of today. Yet, when we look at the way teachers are teaching and the way the school functions, little has changed over the past 100 years.

So much can be said about the art of teaching and impact that powerful, life-changing, good teaching has on the success rate of our schools and society. The purpose of this chapter is to look back at the basics of teaching that Dewey shared in his work. When we compare the basics to today's teaching methods and classroom systems, then we can make sure we are teaching in ways to meet the needs of the students we serve.

Teaching Basics

The teaching basics require three things:

1. the right teachers in place who care and are concerned
2. the right classroom space to teach with tools to make a classroom environment
3. a process to support reflective teaching methods that are child-centered

Dewey shared that the young are the chief asset of our society. It is extremely important to properly protect and nurture young students. Acts of care in the best interest of the young is the most fundamental gift we can give our world. Our job is to ensure our children are properly cared for as they grow and develop.

Children need to be taught by someone that has great concern for who they are as an individual. This is not easy for some adults. Dewey knew that some adults see young children as inferiors and tend to teach down to them. Dewey said that adults who are tyrannical and patronizing should not be teachers. In classrooms today, there are many teachers in the profession that do not have the right dispositions about the young and cause harm to the demeanor of developing students. We need the greatest teachers who care and have the best interests of the children they are teaching in mind.

Once we have the right teachers who care about students in place, next we need to make sure the teachers are given the best classroom spaces to teach in. They also need the proper tools and supplies to create a learning environment and teach amazing lessons.

When thinking about teaching, it is impossible to leave out the circumstances in the school environments. Even with the best teachers on staff, the school environment is directly related to the way teachers teach and the ways students learn.

There is a trending video clip on social media comparing a "government funded" classroom to a "teacher funded" classroom. The government funded classroom is the classroom at the school that the teacher and class are assigned to. The space is often bare with just furniture, a teacher computer, and blank walls. When clips of the government funded classroom are shown, the spaces are in rough shape. They lack bookshelves, bulletin boards, and an overall inviting learning space.

Then the video clip shows what was the original space that has been transformed into a new and improved teacher-funded version. To get the improved classroom, the teacher had to spend her own money to purchase paint, signs, colorful borders, anchor charts, furniture, and comfy learning space pillows. The teacher's parents and family members are seen helping the teacher make the old space new by cleaning, painting, and building shelves. What was once an old, worn-down government room has now become a bright, inviting classroom.

Think about the physical school area and individual classroom learning spaces. Some classrooms are in portable buildings placed around the outside of the main school building. Besides aesthetics, these portable classrooms are sometimes old and built without a personal bathroom. Backpack hooks and storage cubbies are missing. Backpacks and students' coats end up falling all over the place. There is not much that can be done to enhance the learning environment in a small portable building that has become a makeshift classroom space.

What should the perfect classroom teaching space look like today? You might imagine technology on the walls, desks, and everywhere for the teachers and students to access. You might see bright furniture that has movement built in, not single desks sitting in rows. You might imagine a charging station and a library with daily newspapers on display. There might be a robotics section, a lab space for experiments, open windows with natural light, and animals to study and care for. Dewey shared that animals (pets) are for science and humanity.

You might see touch screens by the classroom doors (running off apps) that students and guests can use to check in and out of the classroom when needed. You might see a current world news broadcast being played. There might be access to a small garden project with data collection growth charts displayed. Student's jobs might be posted for all in the learning community to see. Personal self-care spaces might be incorporated.

The classroom space and tools are the backbone of good teaching. For any current classrooms that are lacking, these ideas are not meant to condemn your learning space in any way. For the most part, teachers are going above and beyond to create spaces and to deliver their best to the students. Teachers often have little choice when it comes to the classroom space they are assigned and the tools they are given to work with. There are many excellent teachers spending their own money and resources to build the best environments that correlate to student learning.

Teachers need supplies to teach well. In the past, yearly teacher budgets per classroom were allotted for classroom supplies and learning tools. The budget was something like $500. This money, in its entirety, was quickly spent on chart paper, lamination fees, copy fees, student take home folders, Expo markers, and sticky notes. Anything else would come from teachers or parents. Is it right to think that teachers and parents should pay for the basic school tools? Do we know where all the money for things like up-to-date school buildings, classroom furniture, and the basic supplies is going?

Teachers are clever. They learn to shop sales, hunt gently used books at thrift shops, and repurpose used furniture to make the classroom feel like a home. And as a community, we let them do just that. Dewey knew that together it was the job of educators, parents, teachers, and the state to ensure there is an appropriate learning environment in place. This space should support the proper education and the learning activities needed to support a child's growth and development. Teachers should not be alone.

We must stop and recognize that classrooms are outdated and underfunded. Teachers are underpaid and undersupplied. All these pieces are a part of how we teach. Dewey said that when the school and community become one, teachers will have a classroom space and the proper supplies. This is a call to the community. We must not let this continue to happen. We must be asking, observing, helping, and checking in on teachers often. How we teach students starts with highly qualified teachers who are given the best classroom spaces to teach in and access to cabinets stocked full of supplies.

We must continue to recognize the importance of a teacher with nurturing dispositions and make sure they are provided classroom spaces and access to supplies. Once teachers are prepared with the space and the supplies, the methods of teaching can be discussed. There are many awesome models of teaching. But we must embrace the reality that there is so much that needs to be improved with the basics of teaching and the methods of delivery that are systematically expected.

We need a process to support teachers to plan, teach, and reflect on the methods used. The methods used must be child centered. The way we teach today is so fast paced. Before there is time to think about the lesson and how it went, teachers are expected to move ahead with the next day. If a reflective process is in place, teachers can begin to fine tune their teaching strategies.

It is often observed that teachers tend to teach the way they were taught. Based on deep-rooted incorrect beliefs engrained in our society, it is common to think that teaching (and learning) must "look" a certain way to be correct. It is often expected that a teacher, leading the classroom, should lead in such a way that they produce a class of observable children that look and respond a certain way. This "way" is all based on a pre-conceived idea of what learning "looks" like.

Administration continues to solidify the use of outdated teaching methods that society has perceived to be the "correct way" of teaching and learning. Because of looming, unplanned classroom observations, teachers and students know that when being watched by administration at school, they better look and act a certain way. During these informal observations, administrators document what they see. Evaluating administrators are trained to look for behavior issues, students who look to be on-task, and whether the teacher is implementing the daily lessons they were told to follow. Even though the informal observations are fast (only 15 to 20 minutes long), the observational data is set in stone and recorded in the teachers' record.

Anything during the evaluation that administrators see as a deficit can then become a teacher professional growth plan to address what needs improvement. This growth plan is based on administrator-recommended goals. The goal must be a measurable way to redirect the teachers and get them back where administration think they should be.

Dewey would most likely challenge us to step back and rethink the incredible amount of pressure we put on teachers. Extra pressure leads to burnout and can progress quickly. When teachers are being forced to teach in a way that is not best for their students and have teaching observations held over their heads in a threatening way, the system begins to break.

Earlier in the chapter the classroom space was mentioned. Here is where the space and teaching connect. Based off of the perceived model of what teaching and learning looks like to an onlooker, to "see" the teaching, administration usually begins with an observation of the classroom space. When setting up the classroom, teachers spend days moving furniture around until it is just right. The setting up and furniture position speaks volumes for what kind of teaching is taking place in the classroom.

For the most part, the classroom's furniture consists of twenty individual desks that are expected to be set up in rows. The furniture used by the teachers is what was provided and they are expected to make work. *Did you know that the typical school desk model was designed in 1880?* Knowing it is not best teaching practices for students to be setting in isolation from peers, many teachers get creative and connect four of the individual desks together attempting to create a table. Working in groups is a part of good teaching.

If the teachers and students in elementary classrooms are lucky, you might find a large classroom rug where the class can gather. The carpet space interaction is another observable way for teaching to be seen.

Implementing flexible seating is a trend, but the end goal is ultimately the same. Small learning spaces may be created in the classrooms throughout the grades, but these spaces are mostly made by grouping individual desks and chairs. Small spaces are needed for small group work. Group work is so important to teaching, learning, and transitioning into the world, but the classrooms and furniture are not set up for that kind of style.

Almost always, the teacher has a carefully planned seating chart that separates the "talkers" and seats the troublemakers near the teacher. The teacher knows that they might need to gently remind the talker to be quiet at any time. This is because we have been conditioned to think that learning looks like a classroom of children that are quiet most of the time. The observer checks to see that the teacher is standing up in front of the students and giving direct information by talking. All students should be sitting still, and their eyes should be fixed on the teacher.

Classroom procedures impact the way we teach. Procedures are in place so that every student understands they should raise their hand to be called upon to speak. Any student outbursts observed can be seen as a teacher classroom management error and can be negatively documented on the teacher's evaluation. Hopefully when administration observes the lesson, the students are not talking much (unless they have been given permission), and hopefully all students are awake and alert.

The permission to talk is given by the teacher and talking should only be to specifically answer a direct question that was asked. If the students' eyes are not focused on the teacher and the room is full of chatter, it is often perceived that learning is not taking place. This is contradictory to what Dewey knew about the developmental process of communication that leads to learning.

We know that babbling to a baby is important for development. We often see good parents encouraging babbling because they know this is one of the earliest signs of meeting this communication milestone. We should never try and stop a baby from babbling. Babbling transforms into language and then that language leads to the communication of new ideas and the sharing of emotion. Being able to talk and share thoughts is the advanced level of babbling. Communication is great. Students need to use talking to communicate and talking/communicating should not be discouraged at school.

Teacher observations by administration and what we perceive as teaching and learning look like is flawed. Dewey shared that the child who appears to be learning and doing might not be what it seems. Students are smart. He explained that the students learn the exact amount of attention that must be given to satisfy the teacher. When actually the child is saving their strongest powers for what really appeals to their interests. Dewey went on to explain that while the teachers celebrate the child's well-disciplined habits, it is often not realized by onlookers that the child has no real discipline at all. Most children are just going through the motions to get through the day.

When teaching, Dewey spoke about the tasks the child is given and when observing, the truth that a child has divided attention. The drifting mind at school is focused on what is most important to the child. What is on their drifting mind is what our teaching should align to. We cannot forget what Dewey said about teaching and learning being a social experience. The classrooms previously described are opposite of what society expects of us. Today's schools are not a place to gain social experiences. Schools are very strict controlled situations.

While we think learning is happening, the students can be tricking the teachers and patiently waiting to move on to the after-school part of their day that has real meaning. The everyday basic teaching models we see happening are very much opposite of Dewey's advice that schools should be an active social environment full of experiential learning.

When teaching, the quality of the lesson plan is very important. With the influx of scripted curriculum, most of the lessons being taught today are from a script. Using a pre-planned lesson (written by a curriculum company) is required. Requiring scripted lesson plans allows the principal to flow from one classroom to another and see that all the children are getting the exact same lesson at the exact same time. More on scripted lessons in chapter 4.

The mandates and monitoring of scripted lessons are affecting the way we teach. In some cases, they are out of control. In some classrooms, signs are posted for all to see reminding what lesson the teacher is to be on that day. If they are behind a lesson, it is written on the wall for visitors to see.

An added layer in place to monitor teachers and the lesson number they are on is the implementation of common grade level module assessments. These assessments are given to all classes every few weeks. If the teacher is not done with the assigned lessons, it will be revealed in the classes' common assessment results. The assessment results are shared with the teacher team in a meeting. The class results are projected on the wall and dissected in an intense manner. In some situations, schools in a district share the results with other schools across town (in the district) for building level accountability.

In some school districts, class performances on assessments are factored into yearly teacher evaluation scores. Low teacher evaluation scores can be used to reprimand a teacher. Some teachers may be placed on an improvement plan. To avoid trouble, teachers should stay on track and teach the assigned lesson. This kind of day-after-day system can destroy teacher morale.

Since the lessons we teach are so scripted, where do scripted lessons come from? Big companies sell these loosely planned but strictly enforced curriculum bundles to school districts. Stop by a teaching conference and you will see tables of curriculum vendors. Companies are quick to claim that these packaged programs are built from a nationwide viewpoint of what all the students need. Big businesses who are making billions run these curriculum companies. Once the curriculum is purchased, it is then imposed on teachers and students. Classroom teachers have little, if anything at all, to do with the selection.

Effective teachers are best at educating others. Good business leaders are good at selling things and making money for a business. It is a terrible situation when a strong business pitch takes advantage of taxpayer dollars.

Over the past few years, scripted lessons have attempted to move into virtual class settings. Due to COVID-19, the urgency to switch in-person classes to a remote setting made these purchasable online programs very marketable. Teachers can be disconnected from these virtual lessons. In classes, children spend hours working in isolation on their personal devices. Students can be seen swirling the mouse in circles on the screen and/or plugging and unplugging the mouse and headphone USB cords for fun. You can observe random clicking around the page until a green light of some sort appears and lets the child finally move on to earn a badge.

Attempting to find a one size fits all way to meet students' needs is the new go-to model of teaching. There is a misconception that education in public schools is only fair if everyone gets the same mandated curriculum. Some are calling this Tier I curriculum. Tier I curriculum must be given to the students at the exact same time, using the exact same teaching methods.

Teachers and parents are expected to trust in the system (whatever the system is at the moment). The larger society has no need to worry with the details. If a child is falling behind, the hope is that purchasing a one-size-fits-all computer program will fix any issues. If we asked educators what the best way to teach students is, it would not be what was just described. The same goes for students. If students were asked what they want to learn about and how they want to learn it, it would not be what is currently in place. Psychologists, sociologists, and so many other professionals would disagree with the ways the children are being taught. So why is it this way?

Besides dealing with teaching the subject-matter content, we are still missing the social piece children need. Dewey explained that children have their own instincts and tendencies, but as adults we have a hard time understanding them until we take time to translate them into today's social equivalent. Dewey believed that what we teach and how we teach it should be focused directly on the child. According to Dewey, nature would have children be children before being an adult. The demands of today's fast-paced school setting move at a speed adults think is appropriate.

There is no time left in the day to learn to tie their shoes in kindergarten. In kindergarten, children are now learning to read and write even if they have no idea why reading and writing are important.

Good teaching needs time to plan and reflect. Teachers' ability to teach well benefits from being given the gift of extra time. In today's schools, teachers must keep up with a fast-paced schedule. There is little time left in the day to think about their students and what they need for tomorrow's lesson. There is not enough time built in for teachers to nurture needs and develop questions to boost student thinking.

Dewey explained that building in time for teaching methods that promote discovery will support children's growth. This teaching method is best for children. Traditional teaching styles often remove the discovery experience because it is often seen as messy and does not produce rows of children, sitting in silence, and staring at the teacher.

The developing child has life and growth needs, yet time and time again we see the wrong things in focus. It is assumed that quiet, still children means that learning is taking place in their minds. When the observers look at the teaching, they can check off the list that the children are listening and learning.

When thinking about the way we teach, there are more scripted lessons used that do not consider what is developmentally appropriate for the child. It is heartbreaking to watch students expected to endure lesson after lesson that doesn't fit their needs. Even more awful is observing teachers use harsh discipline when a child is not acting a certain way even though it is not the child's fault.

Often children put in these unnatural situations try their best to conform to the teacher's expectations. The children who are forced to sit in one desk for hours at a time listening to a lesson can be seen:

- sitting in a desk slumped over
- staring into space
- wiggling around
- laying with their arms hanging off a desk
- fidgeting with anything they can find

Somehow teachers are supposed to make whatever objects and ideas they are given to teach interesting to the child. Dewey said that asking this of teachers is a divorce between the object and self. Despite all the teacher energy used to make something sound so important, the object is no more interesting to the learner than it was before. When students have a genuine interest, Dewey knew that an identification of object and self would be evident with the child. Then there is no need to act, convince, lure, and pretend.

We need classrooms that allow movement with content experiences. Dewey shared that children have a natural need of movement. When this is not allowed the child loses happiness and health, and the ability to learn in ways that are best for them. He also shared that there is an order students need when learning. He said that students must

- understand their own bodies,
- then tools, and
- then use movement to make things change.

Without growth and discovery opportunities being given to a child, the impact over time greatly effects their attitudes. Dewey shared that when the body and mind are not allowed to develop as they should, we end up *breaking* the child. The child's body is desperately trying to do what is right for being a child. After being told over and over that the opposite of being a child is expected of them, Dewey warned that the child will break and try to avoid school.

When a teacher has dispositions that are negative and strict, a lack of love for school and learning becomes more prominent with students. For some students, the school setting described begins to feel like prison. We all have memories of experiences with teachers who were incredibly mean and/or unfair. These kinds of experiences leave a lasting impact on a student and make a person less excited to attend school.

Dewey explained that teachers who possess a strong-willed, highly strict mindset with their students may not be suited to teach. Dewey spoke carefully about this kind of classroom teacher, and he felt that those with "high pitched voices and sharp manners" are not a good fit for education. This strict method is sometimes defined as an authoritarian type of teaching style.

We condone a teacher's bad behavior when we say to our children that they need to straighten up and do their work or the teacher will get you! We must be careful not to give the wrong kind of power to teachers that do the opposite of what a child needs to learn and grow.

It is critical that teachers meet their students on common ground. Teachers who have an approach to teaching that includes constant sympathetic observations are more likely to build rapport. Dewey knew that children are conscious of hearts and no amount of pedagogy can make up for that. According to Dewey, having rapport is how adults can gain access and understand what the student is ready to learn. This is what true planning and teaching should look like. Forcing a boxed teaching system, with its scripted dialogue, to be read out of a binder is not the answer we are looking for.

The job of teaching is a calling. Being a teacher is an opportunity for moral and spiritual service. Dewey noted that teaching, when done the correct way, can be compared to ministry in that respect.

Questioning

Skillfully planned opportunities for questioning should fill each moment of classroom instruction. Students should learn at an early age to question and to think. Questioning is a critical part of learning and should be the foundation of teaching.

The deeper level kind of questioning only happens when opportunities to think are given. Teacher planning for proper questioning takes time and practice. Often the levels of questioning expected of students are lower level, basic, and flat. Facts are regurgitated back and given a 100 percent in the grade book. We then wonder why there are huge gaps in grades given in school, but success when attempting to apply thinking skills in real-world situations.

Questioning types of discussion should be embedded in the lessons being taught. Questions should be delivered in a way that students have time to practice thinking skills with their peers. Learning to reflect and analyze problems are critical for democracy. Webb's Depth of Knowledge explains the levels of thinking that are important for students to acquire new knowledge. Teachers should plan authentic lessons with Webb's Depth of Knowledge in mind.

When asked to speak at a professional development in-service, it was exciting to hear that the school wanted to focus on levels of thinking and questioning techniques. The teacher participants were challenged to look at their own content and think about the different levels of questioning that can enhance their lessons.

Some examples of questioning from their lessons included thinking about the author's purpose with reading and the reasons characters were portrayed a certain way by an author. For math and science, teachers were building on the connections between the subject-matter content instead of fixating on the differences. These types of teacher professional developments are great ways to change the culture of questioning and thinking for the entire school.

Children are naturally curious. Dewey shared that without focusing on the child, our teaching will begin to weaken their curiosity and alertness. If teachers are not given the opportunity to get to know their students' needs and individual backgrounds, planning and teaching using effective questioning is impossible. This leads to deaden interests and a lack of engagement in students.

Think back to the student engagement teacher evaluation example. How can teachers be held responsible for student engagement if the curriculum and scripted lessons are forced upon them? When teachers are not given the opportunity to teach to the students' interests, students disengage. There is a breakdown in the learning process. This is unfair to teachers.

Effective questioning and thinking can set the purpose for learning new things. When a student does not want to read, write, or practice math, maybe the student doesn't see the value of taking the time to learn these skills. There are memes about the content learned in school being pointless and unapplicable to adult life. Dewey shared that the child will never truly realize a fact or possess an idea that does not grow out of experiences or interests which they already have. Students need to see the value of learning and how it relates to their real life.

Overall, questioning promotes thinking and thinking creates new questions. These learning opportunities is when growth begins. If the method of teaching in place excludes thinking, connecting, and questioning, opportunities for freedom of the mind are gone. Some say the children of today are lazy and unmotivated. Perhaps the children of today are not lazy but have not had the opportunity to question, connect, plan, and act. Having opportunities to *think* freely comes before any action might take root and begin.

In summary, lesson planning and teaching that include questioning are needed. The lesson plans being taught must plan and support the needs of the students. Dewey declared that freedom of the mind, self-expression, and overall intelligence are linked. This type of teaching becomes deep thinking.

Real-World Pedagogy

In his book *The Child and the Curriculum*, Dewey shares that the most important things to a child are their personal and social interests that happen while their life moves along. Separated subjects like math, science, and health, engulf the entire school day with little connection to the child's own life. Dewey felt that massive amounts of schoolwork causes children to divide their attention. He knew that if a child appeared occupied with a topic that was really of no interest, the heart of the student would be somewhere else. This distance of heart and what is important to the child is why we fail at schooling today's youth.

The pressure of school is real and has no purpose to students. One example is the requirement of students to switch from class to class every hour of the day. Children are expected to move all their things (and themselves) about the school day. Just about the time they are settled, a bell rings and they must pack up their things and move to a new learning space. Each move is to a new subject and is seen as a totally different, unrelated part of learning. The connections are not obvious with math, science, writing, and social studies content.

With each subject taught separately, the children are working in a unique Google classroom. Students have a new virtual classroom and a new physical classroom that each function differently. Teachers lean on these Google spaces (often with little training themselves) and assume the child knows what to do. For students, the management of it all is just too much to grapple with and learning the subject content of it all takes the back seat.

Dewey said that these kinds of strict, serious, school system demands become too formal for kids. Students will go through their day, move their lips, but have little understanding of the content being presented. The required school activities should be a chance for students to meet developmental milestones, connect prior learning, and gain social experiences. He shared that authentic activities that relate to a student's interest and engage them in a whole-hearted way that they can makes sense of has a purpose.

To further understand what Dewey was trying to say, we can think about our own real lives we experience as adults. Getting groceries is a task most adults do if wanting to have food to eat at our home. This means that we must get to the store and for most of us we will get there by taking the train or bus, driving our car, riding a bike, or walking. When we arrive at the grocery store, the real test of what we learned in school begins.

We arrive at the grocery store. Right away we must apply knowledge of social norms (being a good grocery store citizen), money (adding each item to the cart and paying for it), and health (selecting foods that are balanced and can promote sustainability). This knowledge is centered around what personal and social interests we feel are important at the time.

Sometimes if cost is most important to survive, decisions to buy cheaper, less healthy foods may be the choice made. If we have a health need, the choice to buy apples instead of brownies may be the best option. If we are hosting a huge party, the number of items we buy will need to be within the budget and still be enough to serve each guest that will attend.

Perhaps the mobile app that provides the grocery store pick-up service is the most efficient shopping method to use. While some might reason that it's easier to click the items they need while standing right in their own kitchen, submit the order, and pick up the next day, others may find this ineffective and more difficult to manage.

Then there is the new drone delivery option. If available in your area, maybe using the drone delivery option for ordering and receiving groceries is better. The drone option is great if transportation is not available. Maybe using the drone delivery means the grocery items arrive faster than if using the next-day pickup.

Those decisions are not easy at first and take several layers of questioning and thinking. A person must apply knowledge about society, math, and health and to their own unique wants and needs. Then a choice must be decided and acted on.

Teachers should teach content using real world situations that build life connections to problems that students need to solve. Successful grocery-shopping adults tackle the task in a wholistic way, whereas students in today's classrooms are taught content in isolation from their real world. Dewey said that learning in school is like hieroglyphs, it is only when these facts are learned outside of school, in the activities of life that it begins to mean anything. This makes it more difficult to engage with the content and later apply it outside of school.

Today, students learn about citizenship, math, and health in separate classrooms. If there is real-world context application, this is often explored in a 200-page workbook assignment. Dewey said that no book or map can be a substitute for a real experience. It is absurd to think that the grocery store would give us a worksheet to fill out with citizenship questions, math problems, and health concerns before we could get our groceries!

As Dewey stated, it is important to realize that *how* we teach content matters, and educators are being asked to substitute real life for superficial lessons. We need to embrace the realities of the lives students face and use real experiences instead of trying to turn classroom lessons into engaging activities that students will care about.

Dewey knew that not all real-world experiences could be played out, but he did comment on the power of the mind. Imagination is good for learning. Dewey said that what may begin as an imaginary idea is good because the imaginary world can come alive through expression. The idea can connect to real-world experiences. If we can appreciate the child's mind, ideas, and powers, and give them access to materials and resources, what interests them will be made known. Then the child's needs can be incorporated in lessons taught by teachers.

We cannot teach students content and leave out cooking, sewing, and self-care. Authentic teaching needs real-world connections to their lives, otherwise all learning becomes arbitrary symbols. Teaching reading and math in the context of cooking is more applicable to the student.

Without connections, some can learn, but often the learning becomes a big mass of meaningless work with no real understanding of why it matters. In this case, successful students obtain the content long enough to pass the test and sometimes just enough to make it through the day.

Self-care is a necessity. Schools are not focused on making sure students learn the basic life skills. At different stages of life, students have different self-care needs that should be considered in their daily school learning goals.

Being literate is so important to our lives. Most schools have expectations that students will be reading by kindergarten. This is very different than days of the past when kindergarten was more social and self-care oriented. Dewey questioned the age students are being taught to read. He explained that when a child is ready to learn to read and if they understand why reading is important, the task of teaching and learning to read is less difficult.

Teaching reading is a complex topic that is heavily debated. Billions of dollars are spent on packaged programs and teacher trainings to ensure students learn to read. To the point Dewey was making, is it right that we insist children read by a certain age that may not be developmentally appropriate for them? If they are not reading by a set grade, we often condemn them.

Children get placed into response to intervention (RTI) groups and may face retention if not meeting the milestones set on the adult-decided timeline. Once this isolation begins, students start to disconnect from their peers. How can children learn to love reading and use the skill to grow if they are made to feel inadequate from such a young age?

On the flip side, some children are more eager to learn words and their meanings. They have a natural curiosity to connect the sound symbol relationships to gain meaning. Some may come to kindergarten with an advanced knowledge of reading and writing. If a child has the basic skills, they should not be forced to sit through hours and hours of foundational reading lessons that are of no use to them.

Math is the same. Dewey knew that rigorous math expectations are concerning. When young children are expected to use notations, this can be abstract and meaningless. This does not mean young children should not be taught about math. However, it is important to look at teaching math through the eyes of a child. We must identify that everything the child plays with represents a number. The developmental progression of each child and the learning situations they are placed in is important to consider when deciding what, when, and how to teach such important content knowledge like reading and math.

Let's think about teaching styles. There are certain teaching styles that activate student engagement. Teachers should have a reflective process in place that focuses on the success or failure of a teaching style with the students. While content knowledge is important, content knowledge without an effective teaching style is unlikely to impact learners.

A teaching style that includes effective group problem solving is helpful. Dewey knew that group work is one way content knowledge can be delivered to students while also developing their citizenship skills. Students need to work in groups because functioning in groups is part of our democratic society. Group learning is not isolated. We are impacted by other group interactions that have happened in the past, present, or future.

Teaching magic is real. Despite attempts to box up and sell an easy fix-all package, without a teacher, the task cannot be accomplished. There is something special that happens when teachers deploy a simple teaching method and reach students. Sometimes we call these light-bulb moments. We should all be very cautious about who we allow to become a teacher. A person might have the content knowledge, but not everyone has the teaching magic in them.

Teachers need to use their teacher magic because boxed programs do not address that the student has no connections to the lesson. Their mind is separated from the subject matter. Dewey said that incorrect teaching methods are used to fill gaps. Sadly, the wrong teaching method was used from the start. This is a cycle of trying to fix a problem with a new problem. Dewey encouraged a teaching process that looks at what can be done to naturally meet the learning goals.

Shared lesson planning is a big part of teaching. Because of the use of scripted curriculum, a trend of lesson planning by annotating has emerged. There are some who think that teacher preparation programs no longer need to teach lesson planning since the lesson plans are mandated. All lesson plans will be given to the teachers to use. The annotation method of lesson planning is a process of crossing out, circling, highlighting, and adding notes to the lesson plan to effectively prepare for student needs.

While many are on board with annotating, one principal explained that annotated plans were terrible to read and follow as an outsider. What happens to a teacher who has knowledge of the class and their needs and is told to annotate premade plans instead of planning on their own.

Authentic lesson planning is partially developed in teacher programs, but it is also developed with time and teaching experience. The novice teacher has so much to contribute to teaching and learning, and with mentorship, passion, care, and time, the possibilities are endless. If teachers are given the time and opportunity to grow with lesson planning and teaching the correct way, they will not have to force the engagement with students. The desire to learn will be more natural.

With the recent teacher shortage, there have been many new ideas on who can fill teachers' roles in the classroom. More and more states and districts are placing a person with little formalized training in the classroom teacher role. Most schools are required to let the parents know that the teacher of record is not certified to teach.

Is just letting anyone serve as a teacher best practice? As shared, learning the art of teaching takes time. Why is it that teachers are so hard to find and keep? We need devoted and skilled teachers that are prepared to work with students for the right reasons.

Teacher pay is terribly low. The classroom resources that teachers are given is inadequate. Teachers are not respected and not given the opportunity to teach in ways they know are best for their students. When looking at long-term generational studies, there seems to be a different movement with future teachers who are much different than before. New generations feel that if the job they are doing is not of value, they will quit. Leaving teaching never crossed my mind, but that may not be the case with the future teachers.

We need devoted, capable, passionate teachers to lead our classrooms. This teacher magic is not possible for everyone. We need to address the teacher shortage by valuing educators for their expertise, providing resources, and embracing the shared burden of teaching the young.

Leading the Quest for New Ideas

Educators should be leaders in the quest for new knowledge. To facilitate new ideas, there should be an established classroom environment that allows for students to participate in the learning community where thoughts are shared and can begin to grow into ideas. Dewey shared that good teaching needs a culture with thinking space that appeals to the powers and needs while including new material to test, try, explore, and grow. Dewey shared that there is growth in the discovery process.

Dewey shared that students need tasks that have meaning in their lives. If students are given a task to do, they may do it and find it interesting. Once it's over, they may not care since it is of no use. We can think of this like working a puzzle. At first the puzzle is interesting but not of much use when the task is complete. Dewey shared that teachers need to create interest by appealing to other motives. These other motives are how the "teaching" can occur. This teaching will lead to growth of future ideas.

In this environment, teachers should realize the importance of leading their classroom of problem solvers that will change the world to one we want to live in. Dewey shared an example of the benefits of having students think in problem-solving-type situations. Dewey shared a story about a child who is given the task to move a stone. If a learner is posed with the task, the learner might discover that they cannot move the stone. Then the learner must decide to stop trying, keep trying, or invent a way to move it.

Unfortunately, teachers are bound by so many constraints that make this difficult. Some of these issues include rigid observations, mandated curriculum, old ideas of what "learning" looks like, high stakes testing, and a lack of supplies.

To lead the quest for new ideas means that teachers must be given flexibility with their teaching methods and content selection. It is my experience that teachers do not often, if ever, think about how different and better teaching and learning in their classroom can be. This is simply because they are never given the chance to speak out about the tremendous expectations placed on them.

Recently, there was an opportunity to speak to a brilliant graduate class about the future of teaching. We looked at a video of a drone delivery service that Walmart has begun testing. A robotic fry cook was analyzed by the class and deemed efficient. We dissected the metaverse and pondered the future of online interactions for social and commercial reasons.

When asked how they are leading teachers who can prepare students for the near future, the room was quiet. Their brilliant ideas were clouded with all the top-down tasks they were given to do day-after-day. The schedule was so full of stuff that really didn't matter. The saddest part of all, was when we thought about how things could be different. The mood shifted.

When administrators are told to observe and score teachers who are told to teach a scripted content, on a strict schedule, day by day and week by week, then handle all the other extras, there was no time left to look up. How can any change even be talked about? These leaders are never given a chance to speak. These children are never asked anything. Year after year, someone is making decisions, but no one really knows who. No one really knows why.

Decision makers need to be uncovered. These powers need to be relooked at for the sake of structural change. Top-down directives have been a huge cause of the downfall in education in America. It is time we give a voice back to the ones serving and being served.

We must realize that the reason learning is not occurring may not be incompetency. Students can learn, and teachers can teach. Dewey cautioned that when teachers have no voice, and students make no sense of why learning certain content matters, there is a breakdown of the system We must remember that even when content is being drilled over and over, if it is not useful to life, it is not truly retained. Students need to be given the opportunity to question the "why" we need to learn things and avoid the "who cares" mindset we see in students so often. Teachers and students need a voice and community support.

As adults we should recognize that we tend to be afraid that a child will never know what to do in life unless we drill it into them. It is after several attempts of unsuccessful drilling that as adults we often say, "they are just going to have to figure it out for themselves." This same idea is true at all levels of life. When the content students need to know is experienced, real learning can take place.

Teachers should lead students in democratic learning to embrace new ideas, reflect on history, and solve social problems. This means that teachers will need to promote discussions of ethics. Teaching styles should allow debates and discussion of research without imposing one-sided stances on students. Students should see public data, analyze, build rationale, and have conversations with one another.

Teachers should facilitate learning as a fellow member of the learning community. This means that teachers, according to Dewey, will have to see the importance of the social life and avoid situations of stimulus and control that are undemocratic.

SUMMARY CHALLENGE

The purpose of this chapter was to look at how we teach, what should change, and why it never seems to change with evolving times. There are new generations of students with unique needs. When we look at what Dewey said about teaching to the child's needs, we should review what we are doing that is not about the child. This chapter cautioned the allowance of educational businesses selling a product that drives teaching decisions.

When it comes to what it takes to teach, teachers need a voice, and their voices need to be heard and supported by their communities. It is not enough to *say* they are supported; the support must be continuous. It is important to overcome outdated perceptions of what teaching and learning "looks" like. This will allow students to maintain interest and have authentic learning experiences that will be long lasting.

Teachers need to be reflective with their own teaching pedagogy. Teaching students to think for themselves is critical to success. The use of questioning helps form life-long thinking skills that are needed to address problems. A student's natural curiosity should be enhanced by real world lessons allowing them to thrive in real situations. This will help them to develop and learn naturally.

There is power in teacher magic and teacher magic is underappreciated today. Administration should stand up and protect teachers and students from outside sources that make big decisions about what to teach yet lack any knowledge about student needs. Teachers need freedom and should be respected for their hard-earned credentials.

Summary Questions:

1. This chapter shared an idea that it is important to "remove the adult" and seek to see the needs of the child. By removing the adult, what to teach becomes more clear. What does this mean and how might it apply to today's educational system?
2. What are some old beliefs about teaching and learning that should be revisited? What needs to change from the onlooker point of view?
3. Why is questioning so important to teaching? How should teachers plan for a higher level of discussion?
4. How can true social learning situations, like the grocery store example shared, become part of the normal classroom lessons?
5. How can the community support teacher freedoms that are crucial to long-term knowledge and societal growth?

Chapter Four

Curriculum

"Whenever we have in mind the discussion of a new movement in education, it is especially necessary to take the broader, or social, view."

—John Dewey

OVERVIEW

Curriculum is defined as the content that is taught over a set period of time in an educational setting. Curriculum can also be thought of as a guiding part of school to help with the pacing, activities, and teaching methods that will reach big picture goals. The curriculum implemented in schools must meet the needs of the community. The curriculum helps manage the daily school details and serves as the backbone of the learning system in place.

Schools should meet the needs of the students it serves. Schools should prepare them for their future lives within a democratic society. A democratic society is more than a government system. It is a way of thinking, discussing, and working together to meet the needs of our society. In the *U.S. Constitution*, the individual states (within the United States) have the right to decide for the children, who are citizens, what their education will consist of.

The federal government's role is more of a provider who can give extra monetary support to states who meet certain criteria and want to accept the extra help.

There can be extra incentives given to individual states doing certain things that they feel should be rewarded. Supports like the *Race to the Top* grant is one example. There are variations of beliefs about the shared responsibility between the various levels of government. This topic is a big debate with political parties.

This chapter challenges us to think analytically about Dewey's comments regarding curriculum. At the summary of this chapter, we can form some general guidelines about how the curriculum in schools is selected, managed, and what the implementation should look like in our schools.

The role of teachers and students is discussed regarding curriculum decisions. The importance of curriculum being child-centered, connected to life, and engaging to students is shared. Last, what the growing overreach of policy-driven curriculum mandates has done to our schools and society at large is surfaced.

The Child's Needs and Interests

In chapter 2, the focus was about the need to put children at the center of all we do. The idea of keeping children at the center of our purpose remains true when making curriculum decisions. Informed decisions about what should be taught, what the impacts will be, how it will be accomplished, and if it is best for students must be at the forefront. Also, curriculum related ideas should focus on keeping the democratic process alive and be cautious not to indoctrinate.

- Do we put children at the center of school curriculum choices?
- If children are not at the center of school curriculum choices, then what is at the center?
- Who decided that something other than the children are the focus?
- Maybe we do not have a clear focus on any one thing?

Dewey knew that if the children are not the central focus, the focus is on the teacher, the textbook, anywhere and everywhere we please . . . except for the immediate instincts of the child.

- When there is a disagreement among curriculum decisions and doing what is best, who gets to decide?
- Do the state's hired teachers, the administrators, the school board, unions, lobbyists, or policy makers pick?
- Are these decision makers local members of the community that stay connected to the heart of the school and community needs?
- Are these decision makers from faraway?
- Does the decided curriculum practice come from outsiders who know little about the specific students but still have so much influence with the final curriculum decisions?

To tackle these questions, we must get back to some basics. Dewey shared specific beliefs about curriculum. He said that those people outside of the school should *not* be making the call when curriculum is being selected. Dewey said it is the child's own instincts and powers that make up the material needed for curriculum. He went on to say that the needs gathered from the child should be the starting point for all things educational. This verifies that children should be the biggest part of the decisions made involving curriculum and what needs to be taught.

Dewey knew that when selecting curriculum and materials, they must connect to the children's interest. Figuring out what is in the best interest of the child will have different standpoints. Each of these standpoints are probably wrong. Dewey believed that starting with the child's standpoint is the only way to ensure that the right decision is made with curriculum.

A former student shared a meme on her social media. This meme was sharing a conversation between students and their teacher in a first-grade class during a math lesson. The teacher asked the class, "Does anyone have any questions about math?" Five different 1st-grade students responded to the math question with information about a loose tooth, butterflies, their mom's online school, a puppy, and the waffles they had for breakfast.

This is a funny, innocent experience most teachers can relate to. However, there is more to this. Dewey shared that we must connect with students and what they are curious about. If the math lesson could have first connected to the class, the students would not be distracted trying to understand their own real-life experiences.

Children live in a bigger world than their classroom. They are trying to learn what they need to survive and thrive. If curriculum does not cover what they need, school is just piling up their brains with extra stuff. If children cannot connect their needs to what is being covered in the curriculum, then whatever task is being expected of them becomes symbols that mean nothing to them.

When nothing matches in the mind, Dewey described school as being weird and strange to a developing child. It is a concern that students in school are cut off from the real world. The real world is where students must live and appropriately respond. Children suffer when they are not prepared.

How do we know what to teach? The alternative to purchasing hundreds of thousands of dollars in curriculum is for a group to develop a general list of interests that connect to students in an age group or grade level. Then this list must turn into engaging lessons. Understanding where specific subject matter fits in with what the child already knows is the tricky part. How can a list of items align with meaningful experiences the students need to have?

This list idea might seem like a guessing method. The guessing method leaves room for errors. This is because an adult is deciding on what, when, and how certain things are taught. The burden of figuring out what motivates the child will still be an issue. If this is not resolved, Dewey shared that the bright and intelligent children begin to dislike school and what comes out of it. He shared that this can be a real handicap and something the person never fully grows out of.

So, what does a child need? Back in chapter 1, the most basic needs of a child were discussed in great depth. It was shared that it is important for a child's basic needs of food, shelter, and so forth to be met before any type of educational growth should be expected. If the basic needs are met, what else does a child need to know about?

When learning, we know that play is needed for children. When children get to play, there is improvement in a child's problem-solving skills. The next step is to understand the child's knowledge needs. This can be done by systematically getting to know the child. The process of understanding a child should be a continuous questioning process. The child-delivered answers will lead us to the appropriate, relevant, real-time knowledge they possess. This knowledge can inform decisions about planning for curriculum. Then the task of making day-to-day lesson-planning decisions will be a breeze.

An authentic "seeking to understand" model is where the importance of strong teaching methods of questioning discussed in chapter 3 begin to take root. Dewey wrote extensively about the need to ask and answer questions to best understand in all areas of life. This type of questioning process is much bigger than the Know/Want to Know/Want to Learn (K/W/L) chart so often used at the start of a pre-planned unit.

Being a parent of three children, despite very similar upbringings and life experiences, each child has very different learning needs. What knowledge each child needed throughout their lives was different for each individual person.

One child might have a natural gift of connecting to others. This child might engage in conversations with others and have an outgoing personality. This child may possess a talent of sewing and finding all nature-related things intriguing.

Another child, from the same household, can be considered a deep thinker and thrives with an advanced understanding of business knowledge. The child has a big vision for personal direction and an appreciation for music.

The other child has reading mastered before the age of 4. There is an interest in exploring advanced technology. This child constantly grapples with ways to meet the wants and the needs of others in their life.

Dewey shared that he learned so much from his own children. He knew the constant struggle for parents trying to meet the needs of their individual children. Parents of multiple children understand the constant juggling it takes to raise each child and differentiate the supports in life they need.

Ultimately, parents have an advantage over teachers when they understand their child in a more personal way. This is where partnerships between parents and teachers are very important.

Consider a parent-child profile chart. The chart below is simple. However, this chart will open the doors to bridge the classroom teacher and parents. This chart is symbolic of a classroom culture that works together to care for and grow the child with the help of the parent. This also symbolizes the understanding that the parent has so much valuable knowledge about their child.

If a parent has not thought about their child in this manner, this activity is an opportunity to spark ideas and create a new path of connections between parents and children. The simple chart below (Table 4.1) can be life-changing.

Dewey believed that understanding a child is how we figure out what the child can do. Understanding what the child struggles to do, connects to their engagement. Trying to engage a student takes a toll on the mental and physical side of teaching. As Dewey shared, getting to the root of what a child can do and wants to learn about avoids wasting time and energy.

When we first focus our attention on the child, we will help connections to form and give the task value. The attitude of the child will shift. It is important to know that when focusing on the child's interests, it does not mean that whatever the child wants to learn about is the ultimate standard of all that will be done at school.

Teacher Autonomy and Voice

Teachers are experts but are not always treated as such. To be a teacher, years were spent earning a degree in the field of education. The work is not an easy accomplishment. Dewey believed that teachers should be seen as experts and as artists who have the creativity to encourage students to think.

Teachers need the power to promote imaginative thinking and problem solving strategies in their classroom. To teach effectively, teachers will need to grapple with the ongoing changes of society. Whether teachers have independence to do this or are mandated to use a scripted curriculum greatly impacts their career.

Table 4.1. Holt Parent-Child Profile

My Child's Name:	
My Child's Strengths:	
My Child's Weaknesses:	
Goals I have for my child:	
My child gets excited about:	

Teacher autonomy is lost when teachers, children, and the overall needs of society are not allowed to be the focus. According to Dewey, the subject-matter of curriculum should be made into the terms of the child's own individual activities, habits, and desires. Even if the content is selected in a judicious way, it will not be whole.

Dewey went on to state that history, geography, and mathematics are modes of shared personal experiences. When teachers use the actual interests of the child in the curriculum there is a psychological interest that holds the child's attention.

The truth is that teachers have little to do with how the school functions. Teachers seldomly get asked about the courses of study they teach and how lessons are delivered. Dewey shared that there is little opportunity for teachers to collaborate and exchange new ideas.

Dewey recognized that even teachers, with years of teaching experience get no more respect or credit for their expertise. No one seems to bother with caring about teachers' opinions. Dewey noticed the lack of value given to teachers compared to other experts in different fields of work.

In 1913, Dewey shared the seriousness of not including teachers, who are in direct contact with students, in any of the decision-making process. Not asking and using input from educators regarding curriculum that is being imposed on children is wrong. There are layers of details that go into choosing curriculum content, its formation, and arrangement. This deserves teacher input. Teachers' thoughts and opinions hold value.

Around the same time, Dewey shared that if implementing the use of printed manuals that teachers and students had to use, these manuals would come from outside people. Can a stranger effectively know what lessons should be mandated in classrooms each year? It is even scarier to think someone other than the teacher could efficiently plan what should be taught each month . . . or each week. Sadly, most mandated curriculums have scripted lesson plans down to the day. These packages come with detailed pre-made scripted lesson plans and activities. These have no teacher or student input.

Scripted lesson plans are lesson plans written and sold as part of packaged curriculum. In chapter 3, the impact of scripted curriculum on teaching is discussed. They are called scripted because every word the teachers are to say to the class is typed out. Companies sell the same scripted curriculum lessons worldwide to anyone who would like to purchase them. While fact checking the cost of a popular scripted reading program, it cost one school district taxpayers $29,750 to serve 1,750 students for one year. A more recent report shared that another district purchased the same reading program at a cost of $1,618,600 for a 5-year subscription. Keep in mind, these amounts are just for one subject.

To better streamline the use of scripted lessons, there is a trending idea that lesson planning can be a thing of the past if teachers learn to annotate as shared in chapter 3. Colleges have been told that they are not up to date with the new annotating process and that it is no longer helpful to teach preservice teachers how to write lesson plans.

With lesson annotating, teachers are more likely *not* to write their own lessons. This is because teachers would take the scripted lesson and make any notes needed around the words on the document that tells them what they are supposed to read. The more traditional way of lesson planning is a process where teachers focus on the best instruction using state standards to meet the needs of their students. It takes time and devotion to dream up the perfect plan for the needs of their students. Building the plan is part of the process that leads to good teaching.

For anyone outside of education, scripted lesson plans can be thought of like a boxed cake mix. Scripted lessons are like a boxed cake mix that comes pre-prepared with most of the ingredients inside the box. A boxed cake mix has detailed directions on the back to follow. If all teachers use the same boxed cake mix and follow the exact same directions, every cake should be the same. If teachers want to change anything, they could annotate the directions on the box. They are allowed to write any changes on the back of the box on top of the other directions. Making this cake requires less thinking than one made from scratch. What about when the required box cake mix is not any good?

Traditional lesson planning follows a sequential process that teachers use to plan out the best steps to make sure the class gets the best cake ever! This cake may be something created from an old recipe or something "out of the box" that excites students. With traditional planning, teachers are allowed to plan using ways they know will get the best results in the end.

Traditional lesson planning that teachers must do can be more time consuming than the script. That's why teachers get a built-in planning period each day. Effective lesson planning can be very hard to accomplish if the scheduled planning times for teachers are filled with meetings with counselors, discipline issues, extra duties, and parent complaints.

A school board member shared their opinions about the annotated lesson plans that were expected of the faculty. When teachers spoke out against scripted curriculum, they shared that teachers have a simple job and nothing to complain about. Since the curriculum was bought, decided on for them, and completely laid out for the entire year, all teachers should be thankful and just read the manual provided. This mindset is an insult to teachers.

Teacher autonomy is missing. Teachers must be respected for their own ideas and selections of what lesson plans are designed and used. Recently teachers are being challenged for the selection of literature used. In some states, teachers are having to send in a list of each book used available to students. This concern about teachers is slightly misplaced. A real concern should be monitoring the big companies that are controlling education and influencing political leaders.

When school funds are spent on scripted curriculum, there is no money left for teachers to select additional reading material. Scripted curriculum is most often required, and these packaged programs have pre-determined literature that are used. Big companies are the ones who pick what stories are used. How do these pre-selected stories impact the curriculum? Teachers need autonomy over what books are used in lessons.

The appropriate time and place for literature-based lessons about difficult topics, such as war, is often debated among communities that share the responsibility of raising and educating future generations. John Dewey stated in his book titled *Moral Principles in Education,* that young learners should be a part of the democratic society in which they belong early in life to ensure life-long success with morals. He further cautioned that:

> To isolate the formal relationship of citizenship from the whole system of relations with which it is actually interwoven; to suppose that there is some one particular study or mode of treatment which can make the child a good citizen; to suppose, in other words, that a good citizen is anything more than a thoroughly efficient and serviceable member of society, one with all his powers of body and mind under control, is a hampering superstition which it is hoped may soon disappear from educational discussion. (Dewey 1909, p. 9)

There is a children's book titled *Faithful Elephants* written by Yukio Tsuchiya. This book is about war and is considered controversial. Books that are controversial often make the banned book list. When considering selecting or banning books like *Faithful Elephants* to use in classroom lessons, decision makers need to consider the possibilities that texts such as these might be a support for social change and inspire hope for a better future.

As much as we would like to ban all wars, the truth is that wars are *real*. All over the globe, we see the impacts of war. Even those who are geographically separated from a direct war zone, the convenience of social media has given students access to an up-close view of the world in real time. This has increased student awareness of war and the personal details humans are facing. Incorporating *Faithful Elephants* and other similar texts in classrooms is a way that educators can help students learn to confront tough issues in their safe learning space.

The American Library Association (ALA) began a banned book list in 1982 after several books were banned. While the American Library Association does not ban books, they want others to have access to the list to promote a freedom to read. The produced list serves as a resource for libraries and schools to make decisions about book selections.

Based on the last decade of the banned books list in the United States, books such as *The Fighting Ground, James and the Giant Peach,* and *The Giver* all made the cautionary list warning that they might not be appropriate for children. Outside of the United States, the book *Animal Farm* is banned and/or censored in several countries which feel the content can lead to anti-government mindsets that are unwanted based on historical wars and civil uprising.

- Is this censorship a good thing for the future of our global society?
- Should adults ban books to discourage young learners from reading about events like these?
- Could sharing these stories support culturally responsive lessons that can encourage empathy for others?

Even though dozens of books that have been written about war and other controversial topics, several titles are banned and/or discouraged from school use. This can also be the reason some important stories are omitted from curriculums and left out of textbooks. If a textbook gives information about Africa and the role other countries played in controlling the land and its people, it may only be a small part of the story that gives one side of the facts.

Fear that young children are not the appropriate audience suited for topics like Africa and the Congo or even the 911 terrorism can be a deterrent when being considered for sharing in the classroom. Some argue that adults struggle to understand some topics themselves and these are not fit to share with such a vulnerable population. So, when do learners begin to understand war and how to advocate for peace?

If students are allowed to think through challenges and solutions using trade books centering around moral and ethical issues, they can potentially develop solutions turning ideas into tools to make a better life for all. It is through rich literature and carefully planned discussions by teachers that young learners can appropriately engage with texts like *Faithful Elephants.*

Consider the potential discussion from a book study on *Sudoko and the Thousand Paper Cranes* written by Eleanor Coerr. While *Sudoko and the Thousand Paper Cranes* is written at a developmental reading level 40, or 4th grade, this text opens dialogue to teach young learners' connection with the sudden increase of cancer that impacted so many after the atomic bomb was dropped on Japan.

When reading books like *Faithful Elephants* and *Sudoko,* students can develop personal stances about war. Yet often these opportunities to discuss hard topics are not optional with mandated curriculums that exclude these stories.

In the children's book *Faithful Elephants,* the author uses the point of view of the zookeepers to tell how World War II affected the zoo staff that worked closely with the animals at the Ueno Zoo. Based on fear of bombs falling on the cages and allowing the dangerous animals to escape, the story explains that based on military orders, a sad fate for the animals was given. Three beloved elephants named Jon, Tonkey, and Wanly were killed like other large animals such as tigers, elephants, and snakes. This text is identified with a readability level in the range of a 640 Lexile level, 30 developmental reading level, or 3rd-grade skill level.

The topic of World War II is often mapped in the curriculum plans to be taught to older learners. *Faithful Elephants* is geared to much younger demographics. On a surface level, the kid-friendly illustrations along with carefully worded phrases aim to help the young reader understand the alarming thought process the zoo keepers faced when being required to kill the three intelligent elephants. However, on a deeper level, the reader is exposed to the realities of war and decisions to be made during war times often unknown to the current generation of young people.

There are many different positions that can be discussed relating to the following questions:

- Should young learners be exposed to sensitive topics using literature? If so, at what age and grade should learners be exposed?
- Should the sharing of sensitive topics relating to certain subjects, such as war, be a choice left up to parents to teach?
- Is the argument to be made that school systems should be responsible for introducing topics into daily classroom literature lessons to allow children to learn to grapple with historical situations?

Deciding who should be expected to share difficult topics that often include horrific events such as wars and the holocaust is not simple. However, since it is important to ensure that the youth of today understand historical situations to help them be noble future leaders in homes, communities, and abroad, this question should be decided and planned for.

Carefully thought-through lesson planning can serve as a vehicle for sharing sensitive topics with young learners. If teachers are given freedom, they can build lessons that consider developmentally appropriate opportunities to present content about historical conflicts. A new perspective that embraces the past and raises awareness for the future can be born.

Tough topics can be delivered in lessons that include carefully developed questioning. The classroom teacher can prepare the classroom environment in a way that allows safe conversations and helps eliminate a culture of fear.

To conclude, it is important that more is done to understand teachers' roles so the benefits of incorporating texts like *Faithful Elephants* in the classrooms can serve young learners. Trusting teachers who can help make decisions about the time and place that is best for students to be exposed to difficult topics is needed. The possible implications of incorporating texts like *Faithful Elephants,* and likewise, the implications of not sharing texts that embrace historical struggles in the educational setting should be weighed carefully. The entire world is at stake.

Those who think it is a "gift" when teachers are relieved from any intellectual responsibilities are wrong. Dewey warned that not giving teachers the freedom to do what is best will ruin their professional spirit. Dewey shared that teaching is either a teacher's intellectual enterprise or a routine mechanical exercise. Not either or. Should curriculum companies have all that power?

Engaging Students

On almost every teacher evaluation rubric, you will find student engagement is being scored. If teachers are being mandated to use a certain scripted curriculum with specific lessons, student engagement may be lacking. As Dewey explained, students need connections to the lessons. If the curriculum is not connected, student engagement is lost.

Dewey knew that a child's natural experiences, interests, and impulses is all the leverage a classroom teacher has to work with. What a child will engage with is what is significant and adds worth to their life.

Students are grouped in school by their age. We know that all students develop differently. Children need to learn in the appropriate developmental sequence. Students who are already reading should have the opportunity to work with others that are reading. Is it possible to provide students the chance to learn with others if best?

Political Issues

Curriculum decisions can originate from policy makers. Lobbyists, working for their own specific cause, approach state capitols across the nation. There are many instances where misleading information is given to those in power. It is not common to see representatives on a mission to understand what they are being told and if it is best for matters of curriculum. Curriculum experts must be included. There should be voices heard that are not trying to make a profit.

This process is something that is hard to monitor. However, as a community we need to eliminate the power that businesses have over education. While it might be tempting, this is directly connected to the life of our democracy. We must overcome.

This business control has made its way into higher education teacher preparation programs. Professors have academic freedom; yet lately academic freedom has been appearing on the legislation floor for discussion. There are laws in place that dictate what courses must be in teacher preparation curriculums. If professors and their programs do not produce documentation that certain curriculum requirements are in place, state agencies threaten to deem the teacher preparation program out of compliance with policy. This can mean that graduates would not be certified teachers once completing their program of study.

SUMMARY CHALLENGE

In summary, this chapter shares the importance of every school curriculum meeting the needs of the students it serves. Curriculum decisions should be centered around the students and decided upon by their teachers. Teachers deserve a voice in all things that involve their classes and doing what is best for their students.

A person's basic needs including food, shelter, love, and belonging are foundational. Basic needs must be met for learning to take place. Observing students during class lessons, they attempt to ask and understand their school and their personal lives in the natural ways they develop. Their attempts cannot be fully addressed. One reason is that staying on schedule with scripted curriculum lessons is the teacher's prime focus.

The curriculum must connect to students in a way that they see the greater purpose of learning. When students see the purpose of learning a skill in their own lives, the students will be engaged. Making sure the parents are involved is crucial. Parents have so much knowledge about their children and home life. Using the *Holt Parent-Child Profile Chart* will help teachers and parents unite on behalf of the children.

Lesson planning is a big part of students reaching mastery with subject-specific content knowledge. Teachers must use their planning time to plan for their classes' needs. Rigorous questioning is a key component of planning. Designing and implementing types of questions that need to be taught must be planned for in curriculum goals and specific to the students' knowledge.

Curriculum decisions that are influenced by political forces is concerning. We must be cautious of curriculum companies that hire lobbyists to persuade votes that support their agendas. Billions of taxpayer dollars are spent on an unrealistic fix-all education. Dewey warned about the many standpoints that can be political. He explained that putting students first is the only way to educate and support democratic goals.

Companies sell scripted curriculums that schools purchase. These curriculums may or may not be what students in our communities need. Companies make billions from taxpayer dollars. A purchased textbook is full of stories that were selected by someone other than the classroom teacher. It is important to use rich texts that support the needs of the students.

The ongoing theme is that children must be the center of all we do. The curriculum decisions made and then implemented are valuable to the lives of students and the community. Having the right curriculum in place can promote democratic thinking and change the world we live in.

Summary Questions:

1. This chapter shared that understanding the child's interest is important when making curriculum decisions. Do you agree or disagree? Explain your thinking.
2. How can teachers, students, and parents be involved in curriculum decisions? Why is this important for the community?
3. What are the pros and cons of scripted curriculum?
4. How is curriculum connected to citizenship and democracy? Why is this important to think about with the problems we face in education?
5. How is literature connected to curriculum? What literature have you read that impacted your life?

Chapter Five

Futuristic Needs

"I believe that education is the fundamental method of social progress and reform."

—John Dewey

OVERVIEW

This chapter focuses on the futuristic needs of our society. By looking at the current state of education, we can analyze today's weaknesses to prepare for the needs of tomorrow. The way we support and manage our school system has a direct impact on the future of our society.

Major problems in today's schools hold the attention of our school leaders, parents, and the community. Dealing with school shooting threats, school lockdowns, active shooter drills, fights, gang activity, and child abuse are a few of the top concerns. Some states have devoted extra time to work on policies that allow teachers and other school staff to carry guns on school campuses to protect students. Others have added additional metal detectors and school resource officers. Extra layers of actively monitoring all students to make sure they only carry mesh backpacks and clear lunchboxes are taking up time and energy but make checking students for weapons simpler.

With major problems taking the forefront, there is less urgency to deal with the smaller school day challenges. The smaller school day challenges are connected to the school culture and the basic operations of the school systems. These issues may seem small compared to others. Still, they need to be addressed. Not dealing with the smaller problems is the reason the bigger problems continue to occur.

There has been an education-blaming battle raging on for years. We tend to push the problems we face in education on someone other than ourselves.

Citizens live their lives assuming someone else will take on the responsibility to fix the issues schools face. Regarding the state of education, the blame of the problems has been placed largely on teachers and students. The lack of shared responsibility is problematic. Without unity, problems will continue, and the future of democracy is at stake.

When we think about the future needs of education, making sure that advancing technology is being taught in schools might be the first thing that comes to mind. While advancing technology is very important, the future needs that should be addressed are much more foundational.

This chapter focuses more on the foundational future needs. It is important to reestablish our foundational beliefs relating to education and the outcomes we want for our society. For the sake of our educational system, these beliefs *should* be the focus of our goals. For a process of change to happen, it must be accepted that we are not where we want to be.

This chapter links back to previous chapters that discussed problems we face. Issues with school funding, teacher retention, democracy, and community support are all issues that need to be addressed in the future. When we take on these tough issues, we can no longer be satisfied saying "we do that," when we actually have not addressed the root of the issue in a systematic way. For example, we cannot say:

- "We care about the health of students" and then only allow for 20 minutes of recess free play each day to be allotted into the eight-hour school day schedule.
- "We want students to grow up and be democratic leaders in the community" but discourage teenagers from forming a board to discuss ways to make the changes needed throughout their school.
- "We want to support parents" but only offer a parent night once a year where they sit and listen to a 30-minute PowerPoint slide with school data with a follow-up asking parents to pay extra class fees.

We must *continuously* make our day-to-day actions match the goals we have.

The desires of our society should be lived out every day in our schools. The goals in place should be strategic and recognizable to everyone. Initiatives must be evident in the small details of the day. These details must include the way schools are organized and funded to support student-focused needs. Monitoring the basic functions of the schools as a collective community is non-negotiable.

The future of our democracy depends on whether or not we choose to recognize our issues as a collective group and restructure goals to meet needs. It is time to make bold changes if we want to see a future with true social reform.

Table 5.1. Small Ways of Analyzing Problems for Educational Change

Goals	Possible Actions to Take
End fights at school	Form a committee of students along with a variety of student stakeholders (including those connected to on-campus fights) and together brainstorm ways to avoid future issues.
End child weekend hunger	Use the student basic needs checklist to identify food insecurities as a collective. When needed, form a task force made up of students, local gardening centers, parents, and teachers. Together develop a plan for a school garden project that will grow fresh fruits and vegetables. This food source can be supplemented nutrition on long weekends while also teaching others about community and the science of growing foods.
Ensure students complete homework to learn habits of study and discipline with planning	Have each classroom teacher brainstorm with the children what homework might be helpful and what specifically it could consist of. Then students can agree to homework and the best plan of action. Students will have more buy-in.
Get parents to pay additional class fees for new equipment and until payment is received, withhold report cards	This is not best and should be removed from practice.

As a systematic process, the chart above has examples that can be used as a starting point for educators, students, parents, community members, and school leaders to analyze, set goals, and start to develop ideas for small ways of change. Using this chart as an exercise will surface some school practices that are not best for students and for democratic societal goals. When this happens, a decision process can begin to eliminate or change unfair expectations. This exercise can be instrumental in changing the culture of thinking around goals and the appropriate actions needed to better the current lives of students and the future.

This chapter has an overall focus of making future changes that promote students, society, and democracy. There is special emphasis given on the role of schools in keeping democracy alive. A section is included on the importance of teacher retention and ways of change that will ensure we have future teachers ready and willing to serve. This is followed with future ideas to address life's challenges with a strong, supporting community.

Changing Society

Dewey believed that a government full of laws, strict policies, and punishment would not fix the deep-rooted causes that underlie our society's issues. Dewey understood that education is the foundational method that guides social progress and reform. He very much believed that it's impossible to fix all the issues of society without keeping a central focus on the needs in our schools.

After being inspired by his work in Chicago, Dewey wanted to see schools change to become a place of encouragement that created life-long learners. He saw the effects of hard schooling that was not centered on the student. He wanted to overcome juvenile delinquency and build a school system that produced thinkers capable of changing America for the better.

Dewey knew that *real* education is more than just a process of teaching the young and is also a continual cycle of supporting the larger society of learners. Everyone should be a part of the process that it takes to meet the needs of all members.

A point of emphasis to clarify is that we must recognize and embrace that including *all* members in society truly means *all*. This holds true for all members of society regardless of a disability, age, or diversity. Dewey knew that educational experiences should demand freedom to include all and build upon strengths using personal respect for one another and giving individual guidance.

Schools have come far but continue to struggle with special education and deciding how best to meet the needs of individuals. Even students who are protected under federal law still have so many hoops to jump through. These students and their families must do so much more to get the help they deserve. From inclusion models to self-contained classes, the debate for what is right for all learners is a challenge.

There are adults who can benefit from support, and they should not be forgotten. There are several examples that come to mind when thinking about the implications of overlooking adult educational needs. Adults that do not have their basic needs and educational needs met will likely have a more difficult time functioning as a member of society.

There are two reasons for this to consider. First, if an educational, life, or social skill is lacking, it can be more difficult for an adult to do the many things that day-to-day life tasks require. Some of the important tasks that adults are trying to manage can be health related, job related, caring for family, or being an active voter.

Second, a lack of support in school over a long period of time can cause negative outlooks about schooling into adulthood. Dissatisfaction and disappointment can bleed over into homes and societies. Adults can feel cheated, and this can impact others in their family.

Literacy skills are important for adults. A study from Gallup in 2020 estimated that 54% of American citizens from ages 16 to 74 lacked basic literacy skills higher than the 6th grade. The study estimated this to be 130 million adults. With this many adults struggling to read and write, they are likely to face challenges in their careers. They may have difficulty managing needs that are health related. They face hardships when trying to support their own children who are learning skills like reading for themselves.

Many young students have exceptional learning needs and fall through the cracks. If young students have an exceptionality and go through school unidentified, they will grow into adulthood disadvantaged. They are more likely to face struggles. For their entire lifetime, students that go unnoticed can feel dumb or inadequate. These feelings of inadequacy can be difficult for a person's morale. They might recall memories of how difficult school was and the hardships they faced.

Sometimes there are generational learning struggles. From one generation to the next, parents may pass on to their children their personal feelings that they were not any good at school. Many times, parent-teacher conferences become a sounding board for a parent's past struggles with academics to be explained. They make connections of their situation to their child's situation. This is common with dyslexia and other reading struggles. Often parents pass on their feelings of inadequacy along with hereditary academic struggles.

Diversity issues encompass more than age and disability. The future educational needs must give careful attention to analyzing the diversity needs of the community using a global lens. Careful analysis will help make decisions related to educational goals that are inclusive for all.

When a need is identified, all members of society need ways to access the adequate support they need. This help might include their educational needs, life skills, and/or social skills. All ages and exceptionalities must be included. Specific populations that are diverse must not be forgotten or pushed aside. When everyone is supported, everyone can return the help along the way. This help guides future generations.

Society is impacted by school assessment protocols. Often, school success is defined by how well a student performs with a certain expected output. The future of assessment and, in particular, how we define school success must be revisited. There is an abundance of assessment requirements (with attached expectations) throughout the school day being placed upon children. Assessments are rarely taken away but more get added. Assessments have not evolved with the changes in the world.

For learners, achieving school success can sometimes feel like they must meet a quota. Not only do students need to know how to solve one math problem, but they must also solve 100 more of the same problems. Even if students have the skill down, not turning in homework can cause them to fail. These quotas are like quotas in a factory. The idea that a factory-like output is a good measure of student knowledge is flawed. Our schools should not run like factories.

Dewey said that education is often second to industry. He meant that education is believed to be the method used to create new workers that can grow up to continue supporting industrial needs. Dewey warned that society should rethink this model.

Schools that are set up to support the business world are not functioning the way that a young person develops. Yet today, our schools are set up much like a factory line. Batches of children, bells, and quotas of assessments are the norm.

To have growth in education and see a renewal of society, there must be a shift away from measuring school success by a student producing a specific quantified output. The focus of school must center around the human needs. When human needs are the focus, we will have better success helping students gain knowledge that can be applied to their lives in the future. When we teach thinking skills (instead of asking that tons of handouts be completed), new innovative jobs can be created. This will make the quality of life better than before.

Life of Democracy

Dewey knew that what learning happens during the school day was a very small part of a person's education. The entire life of an individual and all that makes up their life, factors into the education of a child. Besides teachers, parents and families of students play a major part in the progressions we make in education. When united, the possibilities of moving toward a future that is more democratic can happen.

Telling parents that they need to be directly involved in the teaching of their child is hard for some to grasp. Some parents believe that teachers get paid to teach and that relieves them of the responsibility. This is not correct. Parents must participate actively in the education and upbringing of their children. It is true that adult jobs and responsibilities take up the day, but still parents must make time to connect with their child and the happenings in their life.

Most parents have the best intentions. Dewey shared that parents have lived longer than their child and have seen the harsh realities of the world unfold. Most parents want better for their child than what they had themselves. This mindset has led us to believe that in order to be a good parent, our lives must be filled with long workdays and fast dinners on the go. Children need more time from parents.

Dewey had an idea about why parents act this way. He believed that when society does not guarantee the security of a job, security in old age, and an education without spending tons of extra money out of their own pockets, parents tend to place an emphasis on having material things. Many parents feel the need to have material things because material things are tangible and might be of value later in life.

Things of monetary value can be a help if there were shortcomings with life. This belief holds true for someone who needs care in their old age. Parents have seen elders they love lose their homes and life savings to nursing facilities that cared for them.

When seeking more education, money can help make it obtainable. Dewey commented that when a child comes from a home life that focuses on material things, their examples of what is important will dominate their lives. This materialistic focus dominates the world of education. This leads to an ongoing cycle.

The need for a focus to acquire material things is often modeled by parents and can be part of the reason why children respond better if offered external "stuff" as a reward. A materialistic focus in the homes and lives of students should be recognized when looking at future needs. Changes in homes can lead to changes in the ways our school systems feel the need to bargain with material stuff to get a response from learners.

If student and parent members of the school are material focused, this can be a reason we see an overload of extrinsic rewards successfully working for teachers. The "get stuff" society is being built into the culture of school. Teachers and administration often are found using extrinsic motivation tactics to convince students to produce something or act a certain way. These tactics can include things such as using a monetary system like school bucks to shop, enticing stickers, classroom prize boxes, and free pizza parties.

The opposite of extrinsic motivation is intrinsic motivation. Intrinsic motivation is the internal satisfaction that is felt when accomplishing goals and activities, whereas extrinsic motivation uses a tangible reward to motivate others to do things. It is important that a student have more of an intrinsic motivation than extrinsic for them to see true value of learning more about a topic and to have a lasting impact.

Let's look deeper into one example of extrinsic motivation. Consider the common extrinsic motivation example from chapter 2: using food as a motivation reward with students. Several times, schools are seen tempting students with an ice cream party for making good grades on high-stakes standardized tests. While this commonly used tactic may seem so harmless, it is not best practice. Besides basic needs issues and the mental stress, using food as a reward is not an intrinsic way for students to gain knowledge.

Many believe that when we work hard, rewards can happen in our lives. For the most part, children love ice cream *and* making good grades is important, right; *notice the output model word of "making."* . . . But what are we really doing to children by offering ice cream for only those who make an advanced score on a major test? Are we implying that food is a reward that can be exchanged for intelligence and that this reward will forever help with test taking?

Should an ice cream reward be a celebration used for the students who are terrible test takers? Should we reward those who have good test taking skills? Should we imply that we only have ice cream when we make good grades? What if the child has a learning disability? Or testing anxiety? Or diabetes? Do these children deserve to eat ice cream too?

Students should be intrinsically motivated. Any extrinsic tactics must be used with caution. True intrinsic motivation can only come when the students' needs are the center. We must plan content that connects to student needs and their future. This content must be meaningful and have a purpose in the lives of each student. All of these things are important to the life of our democracy.

What is happening to the world around us? People say this generation of kids are just not the same these days. Many are at a loss as to why society is so incredibly divided.

- We struggle to understand the increasing number of suicides occurring with children.
- We can't understand why children are not learning to read.
- We are in shock when we see a video of classroom-closing meltdowns that are taking place. It is hard to see a young person so out of control that they destroy physical classroom spaces and send their classmates running to another room to stay safe.

There is a connection between content knowledge, social emotional needs, society, and democracy.

Future classrooms need to review the academic goals that are desired and their correlation to student social-emotional needs. When identifying needs, trying to work toward the needed changes seems like an impossible task. There is an increase in school-based mental health specialists who are being called upon to help more than before. However, things are still out of balance.

The future needs big changes that must start from the foundation. If we ever are to make shifts that will save education and the life of democracy, it is important that we must first agree that schools must *not* continue to function the same as they always have. If we continue to respond to students the same as we always have, we will never prepare them to identify talents and use their passions in the outside world. We should question how schools support students so they can transition to adulthood and resolve problems in a democratic way.

While others on the outside looking in may be unsure, it is the teachers that have the information we need. Teachers have so much knowledge to share about what is working and what needs to change. Dewey believed that a big part of the struggle for society to understand challenges and identify changes that need to be made is a result of the habitual exclusion of the teachers in discussions. When the teachers, who are hands-on with the students every day, are continuously left out, the needed information is lost. Also, leaving the teachers out brings a reduction of the sense of responsibility for what is done at school and all the consequences thereof.

Parents and children have so much to share about the happenings in their lives. The habitual exclusion occurs just the same for parents and students as teachers. The exclusion of teachers, parents, and students, who are all directly involved with the current school system, diminishes the feeling of responsibility of all the negative outcomes that the world is facing. We need everyone involved in the future decision making and this is especially important for the teachers, parents, and students.

Dewey claimed that the life of democratic beliefs and practices are now challenged. Dewey understood that education without democracy is "thin" and could shrivel over time. He was concerned that without freedom of thought, indoctrination would develop. One hundred years later, this is still a very true statement. We have forces making decisions that are systematically destroying our democracy. With these forces manipulating the educational system, democracy can't fully function as it should.

Related to democracy and education, Dewey had a few specific beliefs that are classic and must be resurfaced:

- Dewey said that democracy cannot be political in nature. In a democracy, all people have a voice. To apply that idea with the happenings in today's schools, this means that all children, young and old, need to grow and develop in a school that is free from politics.

Today, it is basically impossible to find a public school totally free from politics. My theory about this is rooted in observations. It is my observation that political lobbyists are a driving force behind some of the educational manipulation we are facing. Huge businesses send lobbyists to persuade political decision makers to pass laws that have the specific guidelines to fit their products.

Companies are selling educational junk for billions of dollars in the form of curriculum and teacher training, each promising a quick fix to all the woes. Since there is a great deal of money set aside for education (in the form of taxpayer dollars), this business idea has played out to be a profitable one.

- Dewey claimed that we are all co-constructors of a true democracy meaning everyone has a voice.

It is hypocritical to say that we need a democracy where everyone has a voice except for the people that have a different viewpoint than we do. Even the educational focused lobbyist has a right to share their ideas. Everyone *should* have a voice, but if the voices systematically lead to the destruction of democracy, each voting citizen and elected or appointed official should approach with caution.

Education is one of the largest money makers. Textbooks, curriculum, online learning subscriptions, food contracts, and more are all about money. The list of stuff that school-budgeted money is spent on each year goes on and on. Look at any curriculum company. Type its name into any search engine. Search and search. Read and read. You will find that these textbooks, teacher trainings, and other nonsense are making businesses really rich. You might even start to recognize the connection of educational spending to political donations and efforts to keep those who remain in power, in power.

This is the type of political influence that Dewey warned about. These companies are controlling the scripted information that is being required in classrooms. This manipulation is an ethical issue that we should be concerned about. As a community, we must question, challenge, research, and follow up on every dollar spent.

- Dewey said that a democracy must be the heart of the people.

If one-sided ideology is taking over all free thought, this is not a democracy. When we think about the schools, we must remember that the school democracy should be the heart of the students. All that is done should meet the needs of the students.

It is up to each of us to support educators who can share the truth. Those who are devoted to the task of continuously analyzing needs of the future and seeing that changes are being made need our help. We must support our educators more than we support those lobbying for changes that pad their pockets. Silence is often seen as complacency, and we must all learn to be informed and speak out.

Dewey shared the need to find out how teachers participate in the formation of educational policies. This is a challenge that was posed in chapter 1 of this book. We must find if and how teachers are participating. The future must have teachers completely involved.

Classroom Democracy

Dewey claimed that more democratic practices should be found in every aspect of education. The benefits of having small democratic systems functioning in every school and in each classroom is woven into each chapter of this book. According to Dewey, having a democratic system means that there is direct participation from all members of society. Our future classrooms should strive to have direct participation from everyone in their learning society.

Unfortunately, deep-rooted beliefs and long-lived traditions regarding how a classroom should function are not democratic in nature. For the sake of our future, there is a need for major school-wide shifts to analyze, develop, and implement classroom systems that are true democratic mini-societies.

There are many specific reasons why a shift to classrooms that are democratic mini-societies is important. The first, and perhaps the most fundamental reason, is that when classrooms function as a democratic mini-society, the students are naturally allowed to be a part of something bigger than themselves. Being a part of the bigger group is how students learn to think about their actions in the spectrum of belonging in a larger society.

Dewey shared that young children need others for support and must learn to look at someone other than themselves. Dewey explained that this need for support is a natural way for young children to connect with others if we embrace it. Since school-age students naturally need help, there is an opportunity to bond with others in their lives who help provide the most basic support. This support is important to the children.

Dewey shared that when small children are developing, it is quite an intense accomplishment to see them be concerned with others. Because the children are naturally seeking connections, this gives us an opportunity for a classroom that supports the building of connections between children and others. These connections will carry over into adulthood.

More than just building connections, classrooms should be democratic in other ways. Traditionally, we think that the typical example of a classroom with quiet rows of children who are directly looking at the teacher and not speaking unless given permission is what learning looks like. Television and movies have continued to use this model for content. This idea of what learning looks like is just not the case. To expect children to learn and develop in this manner is not developmentally appropriate instruction and not what a democracy looks like.

Children should be allowed to speak ideas without hours of direct facts being given to them by the teacher. Many teachers want to dominate the classroom discussion. To combat this, one strategy used is shifting the teaching method from direct instruction to facilitating the classroom. This shift allows students to be heard and limits the sometimes-overpowering teacher. In the future, we need more facilitators and less direct instructors. This need of instruction goes for child learners, adult learners, and all other situations.

To support democracy, using class time to facilitate learning can teach children starting at a young age that their voice has power and meaning. Finding and sharing their voice is a democratic quality that students should have the opportunity to practice. We must change the idea that straight rows with quiet students is what learning looks like in order to save the future.

Setting up a democracy type culture in the classroom might seem difficult. One of the simplest and most effective ways to bring democracy into the classroom is by implementing classroom jobs. There are many ways to make this happen even with the youngest of students.

To start with, classroom jobs should begin by talking to the children about their personal strengths and how their personal strengths can support the classroom community. Next, using a job application process is very effective. This process works with even young children.

When given the chance, children can dig deep to reflect on talents and share their past experiences on a classroom job application. Students have shared that as a first-grade line leader, they were very helpful with opening the door for others. Others who are good at technology have shared their strengths with helping others with basic technology needs during class.

When children are given the opportunity to identify their talents that help the greater community, a positive shift can begin. Teachers and peers can help validate their place and that their expertise of holding the door, helping to manage technology, or tending to the trash on the floor is needed.

It can be rewarding to see children work together and understand the importance of their involvement in the classroom society. Students can naturally embrace their own strengths and weaknesses and learn how to use them for the greater good. Attending school becomes important to students when students feel they are needed.

When using classroom jobs, if a student feels they do not have a place, this is very telling and should be addressed. When students feel disconnected, it can mean that there is a bigger problem that needs attention. All members of the classroom community are needed and should be celebrated for their part in the bigger necessities of life. Teachers should monitor and support students, so all feel included.

For the future, teachers should support students with their classroom jobs. All students need to feel they are an important part of the classroom. Once a student had cancer. This child was often weak, tired, and struggled to stay alert during lessons at times. While interviewing the students for classroom jobs, the child did not complete a job application. Not wanting to give this child more to worry about, the fact that his class job application was not submitted was never mentioned.

The principal noticed and asked why this one student did not have a job on the classroom job chart. After reflecting it was learned that even students with health struggles should be given the chance to belong. This was the best thing to do.

Once the child was given a classroom job and a place to belong, life improved for all students in the class. Not only did the student do well with their job, but the other students were more helpful than ever during times that were more difficult. At the end of the year, the child's parent explained that this was the best year of the child's life. Belonging is needed in the future. We must never forget that belonging is so important to a democracy.

Teacher Retention

When thinking about the future, retaining teachers must be a prime focus. We must recognize that retaining teachers cannot be done by one entity. It will take a community that believes and supports the important role that a teacher has.

First, retaining teachers means that each teacher needs to be valued. Dewey believed that democratic methods with students had made improvements during his time, but the democratic methods were not progressing for teachers. When speaking with veteran teachers choosing to exit the teaching profession, many share an overwhelming decline in value and respect. While we might claim that teachers are valued and respected, our daily actions, or lack of care and concern thereof, speak volumes of truth.

In chapter 3, information was shared about a current trend on social media of teachers sharing video examples of their original government-funded classrooms and then share drastic improvements when it transforms into a teacher-funded classroom. The trend has truth. Teachers are expected to teach in dilapidated buildings. Teachers have a lack of basic resources to work with.

Another related trend was multiple former teachers who were celebrating leaving the teaching profession for jobs that met their own needs. These jobs provided a daily employee snack space where they could help themselves to granola bars and juice. The video trend continued highlighting the new job where the staff could have bathroom time and have full lunchtimes that were uninterrupted without someone begging them to take on additional tasks. Seeing all the comments and likes should be a sign that teachers are tired of feeling unvalued. The future must make changes with issues like these.

Teachers are humans and if we are going to retain teachers, we must begin to treat them like humans with respect and rights. Otherwise, we will continue to see the teacher shortage rage on, leaving behind more damage than society can reverse. The teacher shortage needs to recruit and retain and the basic teacher standards we live by are not up to par.

This teacher shortage crisis we are in is like never before. Teaching shortages have been nothing new over the past 50 years, however the current situation we are in is different and the states are aware. This past year, the state of Florida asked military veterans, even those with no teaching background, to step into the classroom and fill the empty spots where teachers could not be recruited or retained. In the state of Texas, switching to a four-day school week was implemented due to a lack of teaching staff.

In Louisiana, many schools continue to face teaching shortages in all grades but especially in the content areas of English as a second language, special education, math, and science. Nevada reported having over 3,000 teaching spots to fill and has recently sent in their national guard to help cover classes.

What is the issue with recruiting and retaining teachers? At the beginning of the process, higher education programs are the ones who ensure preservice teachers are ready to take on teaching jobs. It is difficult to recruit and retain teachers in teacher preparation programs when they are able (and often encouraged) to just leave the college journey behind and get hired in a teaching job without training. In some cases, a switch from education to seek a degree in general studies allows students to graduate faster and immediately get hired in a teaching position.

For preservice teachers who choose to continue to work on their teaching degree, professors worry that there is an availability of rich field work opportunities that are so critical for retention. These experiences are needed throughout their programs of study under the mentorship of a qualified educator. Today many school partnerships have classrooms filled with uncertified teachers or long-term substitutes. This means that the preservice teacher partnerships are lacking with the needed field work experiences that allow them to observe and fine-tune their teaching skills alongside the highest qualified teachers.

In these shortage situations, often unqualified teacher mentors, who are feeling burnout, or long-term substitutes are the ones with a tremendous amount of influence over the preservice teachers who are visiting their classrooms. Many preservice teachers and professors have reported an influx of teachers in the field telling them to change their majors to something other than education! They explain that the awful working conditions and copious amounts of stress they face make remaining an education major a terrible choice. This is detrimental to the recruitment and retention process.

Online, fast-track teacher programs that are approved by the state education boards seem appealing. Their claims to certify teachers with a quick and fast process have a negative impact on retaining teachers. Some of these programs are all online and mostly module based. Reports have been shared that these programs claim you can become a teacher overnight by watching videos and taking quizzes. These fast-track programs water-down the transfer of knowledge from generation to generation. The passing along of best teaching skills is critical to the preparation of high-quality teachers.

Recruiting and retaining teachers is hard for other reasons. Some get into teaching because they speculate that their dream of becoming a teacher will allow them to pour knowledge into children and change the trajectory of their lives. When this dream is gone, it is hard for some to stay in the profession. Other factors like low morale, little pay, the lack of respect, being overworked, and an abundance of excessive student behavior issues are some of the main struggles to keep teachers. Others claim the overreach of curriculum mandates and lack of teacher autonomy is the main culprit for a lack of interest in being a teacher.

What will the teachers of the future be like? Recently released generational studies are helpful when attempting to speculate what potential future educators might be like. Here is the start of what we know. The current generation now entering the workplace is Generation Z. Generation Zs are digital natives and are said to prefer flexible working situations. They tend to value diversity and social responsibility. Some say that Generation Zs value a healthy lifestyle, and, in some cases, a healthy lifestyle is more important than salaries. Many predict that businesses will need to rethink what they stand for to be more attractive to the future workforce.

When we think about the teacher shortage and the future needs, there are some generation-specific connections that we should make. In a recent discussion, it was shared that the future generation is not likely to stay in a career that makes them unhappy. This is different than some previous generations that were more likely to stay in a job long term regardless of the working situation. We should recognize that the unsettling state of education we are in will continue to make the job of teaching unappealing to the next generation of teachers.

Community Voice for Education

The future needs include a collective community voice working together toward the betterment of education. This collective voice must include parents, teachers, students, administration, school board, elected officials, and all other citizens in the community. This voice must include people who are willing to ask the right questions, understand, act, and follow-up. We need an active checks and balances system for education.

Parents need to have a voice. It should be recognized that parents are in a unique spot being so closely connected to the student. This does not mean that parents are dismissed from the dealings of education. Parents must be an active part of the education process.

Parents should be given ways to visit with teachers and understand what is going on in the daily lives of their children. Parents should be in communication with the teachers often and seek ways to partner whenever possible.

Parents should familiarize themselves with the educational standards that the state requires teachers to teach and seek to understand how the standards are being met. Parents should be careful where they get their information so they can be proactive with questions and not reactive. Parents should also understand that there are forces that share misinformation just to get parents on their side.

Administrators have the next big role. Superintendents, school building principals, and other administrative leaders should be the protectors of education. Dewey shared that administration should constantly protect staff and the students.

Dewey went on to explain that the administration should help set appropriate educational goals. And then, at all costs, guard educational goals, staff, and students. Administrators should not be the enforcers but must be the support system in their building, with the school board, and with policy.

Dewey believed that the administration should encourage imagination and avoid standardization. Administration should recognize that simply completing a list of tasks is not enough. Administration should ensure that students have command of themselves and their knowledge above all else.

The school board has an important job in the future needs of education. The school board needs a voice for education. The community must be willing to serve as members of the school board and attend meetings. Additionally, the community must make sure that the elections are fair and that the members elected have a drive to ensure that children are at the center.

The school board should be transparent and not make decisions in secret. Some take public comments but have a deaf ear for change. Board members should have a mind-set to actively listen to the teachers, administrators, and parents. Board members should visit the classrooms and serve in hands-on roles as often as possible. This is especially true with situations that require the best decisions to be made.

The school board should ask for professional development training for its members and for others in the community, so they can be informed. This professional development should include information about setting (and changing) policies that promote or deny democratic rights for students and teachers.

Training should also focus on minorities, special needs services, supporting diverse learners, and making all curriculum decisions. It is unfair to expect that an elected school board member will know all the details of education. However, it is important that the board seeks to understand at all costs.

The board should freely explain the hierarchical system of communication and ways to change. Anyone should be aware of how to bring an issue to the right place and be heard. To meet all the needs, the members of the board should surround themselves with the best and brightest experts on all special topics. If the school board seeks help from the best, then fair decisions made in the best interest of the child should be simpler.

In a recent chat with a dedicated school board member, he mentioned the hardships he was facing with trying to help make the best school district decisions during such a hard time for educators. This friend asked the sincerest questions related to big issues he is facing in his elected school board role. It was such a great opportunity to be asked to give advice on things like curriculum, parent frustrations, and the process faced with salary increases and balancing the small district's budget.

Unfortunately, it was difficult to help him find ways to solve problems when there are incredible hurdles in the way. His district has little industry and there are low property values. Retaining educators that are highly qualified has been no easy task.

He shared that in the past elections there was no one else in his zone even on the ballot! We need more who are willing to serve in these roles. More people should feel burdened with the responsibility to address the educational issues we face. Taxpayers, who bear the cost of education, should serve. We need their input and knowledge about the community and what changes can be made. No one should feel alone in the battle.

Politicians must be a part of the community voice. Every elected official should have education as the number one priority of their daily jobs. The political leaders should all be privy to the state of education and should never make uneducated decisions.

Political leaders should recognize that there are forces with a sole focus on quietly sharing inaccurate information. These forces hope to persuade them to pass legislation that results in their favor. They want decisions to help them make a profit. Even small pieces of legislation can lead to much bigger movements that may be inappropriate.

It is common to see inaccurate research being shared to political leaders. The misinformation is strategically shared in such a way that it grabs the attention of leaders. Presented research must be fact-checked by many experts from a variety of viewpoints. It should be dealt with in a cautious way so that big companies are not using this fallacy to make money off of education.

To stay abreast of changes, watching legislative sessions and reading the bills related to educational content is important. Looking at the language in educational policy from across the map, some of the exact same language that is being pitched by a for-profit company is being used by those seeking to make money off taxpayers. It is heartbreaking to see such misinformation written into law that was clearly not understood by the author. At times the only people asked to be involved with the formation of policy are the ones who will agree with no opposition. This has to change.

Political leaders should be required to substitute in a classroom periodically. By working directly with the children, more light can be shed on the issues faced in society. Leaders, making big decisions, must be active and always involved.

All other citizens are the glue that should hold everyone accountable to see educational success. Citizens from all ages have so much to share from their own daily lives and experiences over time. There is a history that can be passed along.

Taxes are the way that education is funded and if there is money being misused, the citizens should know. As citizens, it is our democratic obligation to review school records, attend and organize educational related meetings, talk to young families involved in education, and make sure that society is on the right track.

SUMMARY CHALLENGE

The future needs of education are foundational. As a society, the future of education must reestablish beliefs and set future goals. We can no longer blame others for the problems we see in today's schools. We all have a part in fixing the things that are broken.

Overall, family, community, and society are needed for the future. The state leaders, school boards, district administration, parents, individual schools, and teachers on the front-line classrooms need to work together for the growth of the whole person. The small daily actions we live must be critiqued for applicability.

Dewey knew that making more laws is not the answer to fixing educational issues or addressing societal needs. He knew that if we want to change society, we must center our schools around the needs of children. Schools should not be political.

While working together as a community is a big part of democracy, we should not have schools that are solely focused on preparing students for industry-type jobs. We do not need assessment policies that feel like a quota and daily school schedules working on a bell system that are established to focus more on money than on meeting the developmental needs of students.

All people need to have their basic needs met. All people need a voice. This is true for adult learners, those with exceptional needs, diversity, and other unidentified learning disabilities. The life of our democracy is at stake. We need to value teachers and support their basic human needs in order to recruit and retain teachers that will lead the future. We must respect their knowledge and front-line connections to students and families.

Summary Questions:

1. This chapter shared a futuristic need to reestablish foundational educational goals. What foundational educational goals do you think are important to begin with?
2. The future educational needs mentioned in this chapter are just a beginning. What other future needs should be discussed?
3. Teacher recruitment and retention was mentioned. What are some ways that current teachers and possible future teachers can be better respected and valued?
4. Unjust political powers are an issue with education today. What are some ways that educators can work with political leaders to unite in the best interest of the child and the future of democracy.
5. A strong community voice and active participation is important for the future of education. How can parents, teachers, and others in the community build a systematic way to monitor educational needs and support changes?

Chapter Six

Preparing Teachers for the Future

"I believe that every teacher should realize the dignity of his calling; that he or she is a social servant set apart for the maintenance of proper social order and the securing of the right social growth."

—John Dewey

OVERVIEW

Teachers are the leaders of the future. This chapter speaks specifically to teachers and preservice teachers. These leaders must be prepared with the skills they will need to change the direction of the world. The content in this chapter is not focused on the typical ways teachers are "prepared" but rather focuses on preparing teachers for a philosophical shift in thinking about what it takes to be prepared to thrive in a culture of change.

Teachers must rise up to their purpose. Dewey knew this meant that teachers must step into their important role in society. Dewey said that teachers must recognize their value. Teachers can no longer be satisfied with just passing students on from one grade to the next. The role of teachers is not just about teaching content knowledge skills like math and reading. Their role includes helping students to learn what is needed to have a proper social life. Teaching is much more than promoting students through the school system.

We need highly qualified teachers in the classroom. The next generation of teachers must undergo a radical shift in thinking that is much different than their teacher predecessors. A bold mindset that is ready and willing to stand up for the right must emerge among the teacher population. Fighting for the right can only happen after teachers sharply identify what kind of treatment is acceptable for them and their students. Teachers need to know what will or will not be tolerated.

The future teachers must know and defend what the teaching profession means to them and how their role in society must be viewed. This is not an easy task. Currently, the teaching profession is weighed down with decades of wrongful stigmas teachers must bear. When teachers become a part of the decision-making process for education, they can better serve students. The future teachers must unite as one to be heard and included.

When teachers know what they stand for as an individual educator, they can learn to use their voice as a professional. Unfortunately, today's teachers are stepping into a world of dysfunction. There are terrible policies, unfair rules, and wrongful practices in place. Decades of teachers have been walked on as a human being and as a professional. As a society, we must recognize the reality and be willing to ask the right questions, listen, and act in ways that support teachers so they can be empowered to see change for the better.

For so long, teachers have been unacknowledged for what they do each day. For a change in culture to happen, we must undergo a major shift in how society coexists with teachers to make a change for the better. It is the teachers who work the closest with our children. This makes the job of a teacher very important to society.

Throughout this book, there are repetitive themes that have been brought to our attention. The hope is that these ideas will take root in the hearts and minds of the entire world and the process of making plans for change will begin. As explained, to be impactful, society must be united and collectively tackle the needs of education.

This chapter is about preparing the future teachers to be bold, firm, smart, strong, unwavering for the right, and democratic. This chapter is a call to action for a shift in the public's eye regarding all things teacher-related. We are all a part of the process and must unite to combat the unproductive ways education is being handled. Starting today, teachers can get things rolling in the right direction.

Can Anyone Be a Teacher?

The future needs highly qualified teachers. Can anyone be a highly qualified teacher? What teaching qualities do great teachers possess? How are these talents acquired? As shared in previous chapters, not everyone can be a teacher. Teachers need to have a calling to serve, but it is so much more than just a passion. For the future, we want teachers who can prepare students to go into the world ready to face the next generation of life.

Pedagogy is the way that something is taught. To have great teachers, they must be trained in the art of pedagogy. Pedagogy encompasses a variety of teaching styles, manners of written and spoken feedback, assessments, and the interventions used to meet the learning goals that have been set. Being prepared to teach requires an understanding of best pedagogical practices. Chapter 3 shared more about pedagogy and the importance of teachers being prepared to teach with a strong pedagogical foundation.

A solid teaching pedagogy is important to effectively teach the skills students need to have. Having good teaching pedagogy goes beyond having a strong foundation of content knowledge like math or science. It is a combination of knowing the content and what pedagogical techniques should be used with which learner at the appropriate time.

Besides having pedagogy and content knowledge, future teachers should have a love for children and a belief that all children can learn. Also, the teacher's classroom practices should advocate for democracy. To be a teacher is an honorable responsibility that should not be trusted to just anyone.

Society has an important job that we make sure the future is filled with good teachers who are leaders in the classroom. Society also has the important job of making sure teachers are supported in ways that allow them to make the best decisions about all things in their classrooms. Teachers should be qualified, respected, supported, given a voice, and see their value in society. To summarize, Dewey shared that we need respected classroom teacher leaders, who love children, see their need in the community, and are prepared to take on the future.

Dewey knew that the job of being a teacher is a calling. As mentioned in chapter 5, there is a shortage of teachers in the world like never before. Due to the teacher shortage, many states have lowered the standards it takes to become a certified teacher. To fill empty spots, some states are allowing almost anyone who will take the job of teaching to have the job. The job is such an important one and accepting that unqualified people can take on a teaching job is a serious problem.

This idea that "anyone can teach" could very well be the most detrimental decision made by leaders in a very long time. Instead of doing a root cause analysis of why a teacher shortage exists and then taking action to make changes, the standards set to become a teacher just got lowered. The role of a teacher is not for just anyone and the tactic of simply lowering the standards to fill classrooms is not acceptable. Teachers are the closest people to our children and only the best will do.

High expectations should be non-negotiable when we prepare and hire teachers. The traditional pathway of becoming a teacher has high standards for its completers. Teacher preparation programs require the completion of several successful semesters in their accredited program. The programs are chocked full of both content knowledge (math, science . . .) and pedagogy courses (how to teach). Additionally, the teacher-specific pedagogy classes include preparation on the foundational learning needs of:

- understanding how to create and manage a classroom climate
- planning developmentally appropriate lessons and best teaching practices related to special education to support exceptional learners
- mastering special area classes that focus on how to teach reading, assess student's understanding, and support diversity

Just attending these courses is not enough. To become a teacher, there is a set expectation that specific course work is completed at a proficient level. Teacher candidates' grade-point-averages cannot be low. Preservice teachers must have passed standardized assessments (often mandated by law) that prove mastery of both pedagogy and content knowledge.

Attitudes in classrooms matter. To become a teacher, preservice teachers must demonstrate that their professional dispositions are in good shape. Attitude, professionalism, the ability to communicate effectively, and serve others are all assessed. This assessment is not just in the college classroom setting, but it is also assessed in years of observations spent in real school settings.

The hands-on work with school partners is documented and reported. When the candidate is practice teaching in their residency, experts observe the lessons. The experts critique their teaching practice and make comments for growth. Future preservice teacher lessons are re-observed, looking for growth improvements. All of this is to be reflected on.

Preservice teachers, in rigorous programs, must have a variety of teaching experiences with diverse student populations before having a classroom of their own. The experiences take place over years of course work. These diverse placements must include high performing schools, low performing schools, and schools serving second language learners.

Today, there are many fast-track programs that reduce the time and steps it takes to become a certified teacher. Rushed teacher education certification programs should be cautioned. For a person to fully develop content knowledge and teaching pedagogy takes time. Someone learning to be an effective teacher needs time to observe, practice, and reflect on the art of teaching. The process to learn to teach is a gradual, developmental experience. This process helps preservice teachers reach a highly qualified status. Overall, there are no fast-track ways to learn all things it takes to be a teacher. The process of becoming an effective teacher takes time.

As shared, strong programs that create teachers are carefully built and continuously improved upon. Those who are preparing teacher candidates are carefully monitored by other outside experts. Institutions of higher education must pass rigorous evaluations to be an accredited teacher preparation provider. Without accreditation, colleges can lose their capability to graduate candidates who can go on to obtain a state teaching license.

College accreditation teams must prepare for program evaluations and prove (with data) that high-quality teaching and learning is occurring throughout the teacher preparation program. This is true for both the preservice teacher candidates and for the pre-k–12 students they work with over their semesters of study. These accreditation reports are followed up with rigorous on-site visits that include interviews with completers and requested data reporting on multiple educational domains.

To graduate with a teaching degree is a huge accomplishment. The recent movement to certify more teachers by allowing shortcuts is frustrating. It is further frustrating and unfair to have to deal with the effects of such an absurd idea. To think that the best remedy for a teacher shortage crisis is to allow an unqualified person to simply step into the teacher role is a systematic breakdown that is causing societal damage. *To note, it is understood that students need supervision while at school. We must realize that the lack of teachers willing to serve in classroom positions is a much larger problem. Addressing the issues is way overdue and lowering the standards will not fix the situation.*

The teachers in our classrooms should be equipped to face the future. By not having qualified teachers, we are not adequately preparing for the future. We need classroom teachers who are highly qualified and have proven their strong teaching credentials. Dewey knew that it was the responsibility of the educators to teach and lead a democratic school with special kinds of experiences students can grow from. Just being in a teacher role and given a set of students is not enough.

Not having the best teachers in place impacts:

- students
- preservice teachers
- democracy

Student Impact

Young students who are assigned a teacher that has not been formally prepared are not given an equal chance compared to their peers. As shared, to become a highly qualified teacher there are many preparation milestones that must be achieved. Fast-track programs lack quality throughout critical milestones needed for teaching and learning.

Assigning someone who does not have a love of teaching and patience when dealing with the young can take a toll on students' academics and their mental health. As shared in chapter 2, students' lives are already hard enough. It is a mistake to have an unqualified, negative person with so much influence, influencing students for eight hours each day.

Dewey stated that we need teachers who have a natural love of contact with children. He reminded that for some, the contact with the young is a burden; this type of burden often does not work itself out. Dewey also knew that teachers should be smart. They need to possess the skills to pass knowledge on to their students. The teacher is not in the school to impose certain ideas or to make children behave a certain way. The teacher's role is to serve as a member of the community, protect the child, monitor influences (which can affect the child), and assist children in learning how to respond to life.

Teachers should be life-long learners themselves. They have a tremendous responsibility to the community. Teaching is something that dedicated citizens have made an oath to do. The idea that there is no preparation needed or that a "fast track" teaching certificate will suffice is not best practice. To summarize, it is important to recognize that unqualified teachers in classroom positions have a tremendous impact on students.

Preservice Teacher Impact

Besides students, unqualified teachers have an impact on preservice teachers. The need for highly qualified teacher role models, who can work with future teachers, is important. Preservice teachers need role models to learn from and opportunities to see good modeling take place in the classroom. This opportunity is made possible when there is a strong partnership between higher education professors and local schools. These partnerships allow for classroom observations and co-teaching experiences to occur. Strong teacher role models help create other strong teachers. Professional learning communities between all educators is the end goal.

Maintaining partnerships with strong, well-prepared teacher role models is valuable. These partnerships between higher education and local schools can suffer when unqualified teachers are placed in the classroom. If there is no one to mentor, connecting preservice teachers in a classroom becomes difficult.

Without strong partnerships, retaining preservice teachers in teacher programs becomes a struggle. Many change their mind about becoming a teacher. If preservice teachers don't complete their teacher education programs, there are less highly qualified teachers who graduate to fill the classrooms.

When observing highly qualified teachers, as opposed to those without proper preparation, differences can be seen. Often the preservice teachers pick up on the differences between the levels of experience. Lately, it has been more difficult to partner with school teams because more teachers on the staff are unqualified.

Unqualified teachers need more help with their teaching job. Other teachers should not be burdened with tending to a fellow colleague that has no formalized teacher preparation and little foundation knowledge of what to do in their position. Teachers should help one another, but someone with little (or no) training can bring down a team. This takes away time with their students. It can also deter highly qualified teachers' willingness to offer outreach opportunities to support preservice teachers. Overburdening teachers can cause division among staff, leading to teacher burn-out and make retaining teachers more difficult.

As discussed, making it through all the college work it takes to receive any degree is not simple. When the course work gets challenging, the option to quit college can seem enticing. More than ever, preservice teacher candidates are deciding to drop out of the teaching program to graduate faster. This can happen if they switch majors to general studies and apply for a position with a school. Often professors are asked by preservice teachers if continuing as an education major is worth sticking out. Some who decide to change their major and get jobs recruit others to follow their path. When they are told they can step directly into a paid teaching job, that sounds better than all the college courses work that they are required to do.

The preservice teachers, who end up staying the course, feel discouraged by the entire system. They see young people like themselves getting teaching jobs without doing all the work. They have reported feeling cheated.

Besides teachers they are working under, many other educators in the community tell preservice teachers to change their major because teaching is not a good job to have. We need the best teachers in our classrooms that can cheer on the future. Strong, dedicated teachers are needed to support both their young students and the future teachers. Negative experiences like the ones shared have an enormous influence on preservice teachers and the recruitment and retention of educators for the years to come.

Democracy Impact

For the sake of democracy, the future of our society is being set up to fail when we have less than the best teachers in classroom positions. Prepared teachers are adept to juggle many things that go along with teaching and learning that take place at the same time in a classroom. Teachers manage the:

- classroom environment
- workstations
- assessments
- announcements
- direction of outside support specialists and aide staff
- pacing of the schedule
- other student needs

Unprepared teachers will find that their patience will be tested quick. When unskilled and unprepared to do the work the job requires, frustration can happen. These situations can negatively impact the students.

When we allow teachers who are not qualified to serve as leaders, the first major problem that arises is with the classroom environments. First, working groups and maintaining teaching can become a managerial nightmare. Also, often behavior issues begin because well-organized classroom climates and student procedures were not established. Class climates and student procedures must be set up. When classroom environments are not thriving, learning lacks.

If the proper preparation courses are skipped over, trouble arises. Ill-equipped teachers can be observed teaching in survival mode. When in survival mode, a person's responses to situations can be reactive. In survival mode, little content learning or social emotional growth will be accomplished. There is a lack of community and missing procedural structures.

We must value high quality teachers and support their path to grow their content knowledge and pedagogical development. These well-established teachers will be ready to lead the future. We must except nothing less than the best educators in our classrooms.

We must realize that not everyone can teach. Special attention should be given to supporting teacher preparation efforts and help focus on the recruitment and retention of teachers. The standards should not be lowered. Lowering of the standards only proves that there is a lack of value on education and the democracy we all want to belong to.

Teachers at the Table

To prepare teachers for the future, teachers must know that they must be a part of the educational decisions that are being discussed. Teachers must be included, listened to, and supported with any decisions that are being made regarding the students they are expected to serve. No exceptions.

In chapter 1, a challenge was given to ask teachers if they feel included with big educational decisions being made by policy makers. Reviewing the way the school is structured, teachers (and students) are told what to do instead of being a part of the discussions. The future needs a system that continuously centers around teachers (and children) when decisions are being decided on.

The current decision-making system allows for a small group of people at the top to make all the decisions for the majority. As shared, experts need to be involved in the process. In some cases, teachers and others are asked to serve on educational committees. With almost every opportunity to serve on widescale educational committees, the major decisions were already made before arriving. When serving, it was expected that teachers would "check the box" so that the matters being discussed would have technically gone to a committee for review, but the truth was that this representative was not really a part of the decision-making process. The meeting was set up to get the results that were wanted within the law or other policy mandate that was being imposed.

Still, being asked to serve or to give input to help make decisions is not common. Dewey boldly questioned why this backward mindset exists. Dewey knew the effects the exclusion has regarding the professionalism of teachers and how they are treated.

Dewey questioned why teachers are talked down to, and why we think that teachers should be constantly preached at. Why do teachers and others in the community allow this kind of treatment to happen? The preaching to teachers and constantly urging them to do things a certain way makes no sense when you are working with professionals. Today, we still see this teacher preaching mentality occur daily in school systems.

Qualified teachers know what they have been trained to do. After all, they went through years of rigorous steps to become an expert. Dewey explained that the professional spirit of teachers is seriously undermined by the way the school systems are structured. The system is continuing to make sure teachers remain voiceless.

Teachers, according to Dewey, must judge their students in an impartial manner different than parents do. Teachers are not as emotionally involved as parents. Because of this, teachers can give an honest viewpoint of a student's strengths and weaknesses.

Teachers have something special to give about the student that even the parents are not able to do. Because of the teacher's unique insight about student needs, teachers must be at the center of the decision-making process when wanting to make changes in the best interests of the child.

Dewey gave the example of teachers being treated like short-order cooks. Teachers are constantly being asked to fill educational orders using pre-packaged lesson plans just like being asked to bake a cake using only a boxed recipe. Dewey went on to say these *cooks,* or teachers, face the constant task of making the required pre-packaged product they are told to use and make it appealing to the students. After some time of being treated this way, the joys of teaching start to fade.

For the future, we must prepare teachers to stand against systems of exclusion and demand that their voice be heard. Teachers should be allowed to do the work of teaching without being held back by unnecessary rules, regulations, and policies they had no voice in to begin with.

Teacher Support

When thinking about preparing teachers for the future, we must give teachers our unwavering love and support. Future teachers need to know that they always have support and are not alone. There are four kinds of support that teachers need:

- support with supplies
- help meeting basic student needs
- freedom to do what is right for their students
- care for themselves

Many parts of these four topics have been discussed through the lens of the child or the school day, but it is important to bring these four areas of need into the future as teachers are being prepared.

Teachers need support with supplies. New teachers need to be prepared with the knowledge that they will need supplies and that getting supplies is something that requires help. Way too often teachers try to get all the supplies they need on their own. Teachers must be prepared to ask for help with supplies and learn to share the heavy load with others.

Teacher salaries are low, and they should not be expected to pay for basic supplies. In chapter 5, the story shared about the government-funded classroom is a very common experience that teachers face. While we applaud the teachers who do all kinds of extra work like buying extra paint and furniture, it is simply not right that it has come to this kind of life for teachers.

Furthermore, teachers should not have to beg parents, write letters to companies, or build an online fund me campaign for books and supplies. Pencils, tissues, and hand soap should be included with the job. Each year, teachers are expected to ask parents to purchase long lists of basic school supplies. The supplies should be seen as part of the basic needs that come with a classroom. If you work for a furniture shop, should you have to bring your own wood?

Also, asking teachers to hound parents and students for class fees is in the same category of insisting that students sell chocolates and collect box-tops. All these pressure-filled school fund raisers are unethical. What other government-funded program asks the people it is supposed to serve to sell chocolates and wrapping paper for the basic needs? Can you imagine if political leaders were asked to provide tissues and hand soap for the legislation to use for an entire year? Can you imagine if they were asked to sell chocolate bars for office equipment? We would not ask this of anyone else other than teachers and students, and it must stop with schools immediately.

The issue of supplies and money is also true with extra-curriculars. Many students recognize that they cannot afford band instruments, athletic shoes, the cost of cheer camp, or robotics club fees. Many choose not to even attempt to be involved. The pressure of money causes so many students to lose out on opportunities to participate in something that can change their entire life. When even the smallest fees are set, this can add up and become an enormous cost. When a family has three kids in school and each has several unique activities, a $5 fee can quickly become $100.

Some think that teachers are given classroom supply budgets. In my experience, the classroom budget given each year was never more than $500. While $500 sounds great, most of this money was spent before it ever made it to me. One hundred dollars went to lamination supplies. Another hundred went to copying needs. Another hundred went to school-wide folders to communicate with parents. The other two hundred was spent on Expo markers and paper. Do any other businesses ask their employees to pay for the copies they make that they need to work with? That idea seems ridiculous. However, this kind of treatment is common in schools and our society does nothing to change it.

Moving on from supplies, we must think about other needs. Teachers need help with the basic needs discussed in chapter 1. Our communities are rich with knowledgable people who can do so much to help with food, shelter, safety, belonging and so on. You might have seen some community support like this happen with a back-to-school haircuts for kid's event, a fill the bus school supply drive, or parent-teacher events like doughnuts with dads and muffins with mom. These types of needs are year-round.

To prepare for the future, teachers need to know how they are to maintain their freedom to teach the way they know it is needed. Dewey shared that schools, districts, and other leaders should show respect for ideas and experiences that teachers have to offer. Without respect being shown, schools will be a place of mechanical routine.

Dewey commented on teachers having the freedom to think of their classes like life groups that develop the body, mind, and spirit. The facilitation of play to practice problem-solving and allowing bodily movement and exploration of the senses would be best. If teachers are not given the freedom to integrate play and when movement is not allowed, we see a lack of desire to learn. We see students who are lost and difficult to motivate to do anything. This is not an easy task and teachers need to have a well-developed handle on their own pedagogy and advocating for freedom to do what is needed to make this happen.

Dewey shared that teachers must make things interesting to reach students. As discussed in chapter 4, teachers are often told what and when to teach. The future needs teachers who are not programmed to read from a script but empowered to teach authentic lessons that meet the needs of their students.

This means that the subjects and activities must be carefully selected to relate to the students' present interests and needs. Future teachers need to be prepared to actively seek the needs of their students and plan for their purpose.

Going back to the relationship between higher education and local schools, school systems continue to tell preservice teachers that they will only need to read a script and will never need to know how to write lesson plans like they are taught in college. This is a disadvantage to preservice teachers. Preservice teachers become torn between a school they want to get hired at and being told they need to write lesson plans to authentically meet their students' needs.

Dewey wrote that when teaching new material, it must be presented in a way that children appreciate it and connect it to what is important. This is not possible in a packaged program. Scripted lessons are the opposite of new material that children can appreciate and connect to their own lives. Future teachers must be prepared to combat scripted mandates and advocate for lesson planning with the student's needs in mind.

When planning for the future, teachers need to have access to resources and feel supported with their own mental health needs. A recent research article published focused on a college-level class activity to teach about young students' mental health needs. A mental health expert was invited to the class to facilitate the lesson. It was discovered that the preservice teachers were facing their own struggles with mental health, and this made it almost impossible for them to identify and meet the basic needs of their own students.

Teachers face many things that can rip a heart and mind to pieces. Some of these stories have been shared in this book. No one wants to bear these burdens alone or the worse, be criticized for trying to manage what they know is best.

A study in 2019 shared that more and more often teachers are being prescribed medication for depression and anxiety. Teachers are expected to bear the burdens of others when they have human needs too. During the school closings throughout the pandemic, teachers were facing their own issues with health and families. Yet teachers were expected to somehow push all their personal needs aside and continue to do what they had always done despite all the hardships.

During the COVID-19 outbreak, teachers were expected to continue to teach at all costs. The need to tend to their own families was second. Like many others, teachers had young babies, elderly parents they were caring for, and for some, worries about their own compromised immune systems. After being criticized for wanting to stay isolated, one teacher being interviewed said that COVID-19 was different than the normal health risks she faced coming to work everyday.

The teacher said that she always accepted the possibility that she might lose her life to a school shooting and was ready to die for her students. The caveat was that although she was always willing to take a bullet for one of her students if needed, she was now having a hard time being asked to bring the bullet home to potentially harm her family. She was referring to being exposed at school and the risk of taking the virus home where loved ones were staying.

Teachers get very few sick days each year. Most times, they get something like a total of four days. When teachers were exposed to dozens of children, they were being quarantined more often than other professionals. Teachers were asked to use every day stored in their sick bank if they wanted to be paid. It was heart breaking to see the way teachers were treated.

If you are a teacher, you probably know what kind of crazy a Friday afternoon bus duty can bring. Friday afternoon bus duties were the toughest. Students' behaviors were so strange. Friday bus duty was the last task assigned for the week. Each Friday, the wish was that things would go smoothly, so packing up the classroom and head home could begin. Problems on the buses including fights, yelling, refusing to move, hurting themselves, and so much more seemed to unfold each Friday afternoon.

After years of dealing with the most terrible Friday behaviors, it was a high school student who revealed what the issues were all about. This student got in a fight with the bus driver. She refused to take instructions and pushed the driver while he sat in his seat. As the teacher on duty, the radio call for help came to me.

By the time help made it down to that bus, the student was coming off the bus and down the steps. She was throwing her backpack out the door as well as her books, and folders full of papers. All her things went flying in the wind. Instead of getting mad, the response was to just begin to pick up her things and start to put her stuff back together. The girl looked at me with the strangest face. This was not what she expected me to do.

It was a priority to find out if she was okay and if there was anything that could be done to help her. *From the results, it seemed like no one had ever asked her that before.* This student burst into tears as she began apologizing to me and the bus driver. She wiped her face several times as she helped finish picking up her things from the sidewalk. She looked at me and said she was so sorry for acting that way . . . but she explained to me that going to jail on a Friday afternoon was better than going home on a bus to start a long weekend where she was being sexually abused by her father. The look she gave when glancing my way from the back of the police car is etched in my memories.

Teachers face hard stuff. Teachers lose students to cancer, deal with child abuse situations, see students who self-harm, and those who live in poverty, or are homeless. This takes a big toll on the mind. Mental health needs for all humans is an important issue. To prepare teachers for the future, we need to support teachers who face mental health struggles. Teachers need to be well themselves if they are going to pour into others.

Teacher Voice

Dewey believed that the teaching profession should be filled with teachers who recognize the enormous amount of responsibility they have to the public. Teachers have such an important job, and they need to know how important their work really is. A few of today's teachers have a strong voice and actively use it to make change. As a society, we should make teachers feel that their voice matters.

To start, we need a shift in the way we view teacher voice. Teachers need to be prepared to use their voice and not feel bad for doing so. Society needs to take action to be better listeners and support their outcries. Our teachers feel silenced and defeated instead of standing united as the strong professionals they are. Dewey believed that teachers are missing their professional spirit because they are hardly ever called upon to share, make decisions, or be a professional.

Current teachers need support finding and using their voice because for so long there has been a lack of respect for hearing what teachers have to say. We must ask and seek to understand the situations teachers are facing and constantly give encouragement. Likewise, teachers need to seek out their own ways to speak up. Teachers should not have to fear harsh evaluations and write-ups for speaking their truths. We need expert viewpoints, and their ideas should be appreciated.

Looking to the future, we need to encourage teacher voice early in the teacher preparation programs. Preservice teachers should be prepared before stepping into their classroom positions to identify their voice. Preservice teachers should expect that they will need to continuously share their voice with others even when it is not popular. Dewey shared that if there are times that political influences are overbearing with the teacher voice, those who aspire to teach should question their own integrity to stand up against the influence. Teachers are a strong kind of people.

One assignment that is commonly used in teacher preparation programs is the writing of a personal teaching philosophy. This philosophy assignment is the preservice teacher's chance to put into words their beliefs about teaching, learning, and their place in it all. These finished philosophies are so wonderful. They often share words about meeting the whole-child needs, understanding different learning styles, families, communities, and being a life-long learner.

An amazing principal gave their faculty time to revisit their personal philosophies each year. When revisions were complete, the teachers were encouraged to post them outside their classroom door. Anyone passing by could see a culture of care for the job of being a teacher.

Students, parents, fellow educators, and the community need to know what teachers believe and see their beliefs come alive in their actions. We must all live our lives in a way that everyone knows our eternal truths. Let's bring back the teaching philosophy declarations at all stages of teaching.

The future preservice teachers will need to see mentors who are sharing their voices and seeking needed change. Strong communication and having a plan to meet goals shared between teachers and the community is not something extra; it is the heart of success.

Teacher Value

Teachers need to feel valued as a human being, as a professional, and a member of society. Looking at generational studies and behaviors, it seems that the future generation of educators are not like the previous. While there are a majority of teachers currently in classroom positions who are classified as Millennials (born from 1980 to 1995), members of the Generation Z group (born from 1995 to early 2000) are beginning to graduate and find jobs. We are starting to understand that Generation Z has a very different outlook of work.

Generation Z expect jobs that they feel have worth. They will compare the job's worth to the amount of stress and anxiety they face doing it. Some believe that Gen Zers are willing to work hard but only for the right pay. They want work-life balance, mental health benefits, and flexibility. They want to work for companies that align with their personal mission and vision. All these requests are things that the current state of teaching is not good at offering.

As shared throughout each chapter, the basic human needs are very important, and the new generation may not be as tolerant as their parents. Gen Zers seem to have learned from their life-observations what work burnout looks like, and they are not willing to participate. Many Gen Zers are beginning to walk away from employers if they feel their needs are not being met. This detail could be a huge factor in the recruitment and retention of teachers. This generation is not afraid to quit and try something new that better suits their life.

Knowing about generational changes and what they stand for, it seems crazy to say that today we still need to work on making sure our teachers have bathroom breaks and uninterrupted time to eat their lunch.

Preservice teachers are experiencing the effects of the teacher shortage. They are being pulled in to take over empty classrooms before they are ready. We should worry if preservice teachers are in and are prepared for positions, and we see that teacher basic needs are not being met. If they feel overworked and underpaid, they may choose another career. We cannot continue to show the world that we lack value for our teachers.

As shared, higher education partnerships play a big role in the future of teachers. One issue that must be shared is the overreach in laws and mandates that has devalued professors who prepare the preservice teachers. More than ever, big companies are finding ways to convince policy makers that adding new laws and policies will fix the issues that plague the world. Professors are being put down for trying to stand up for balance and demand decisions made be based on authentic research. Sadly, if teacher preparation programs want to remain accredited, the programs must follow their mandates.

Many professors and others in higher education are defenseless when they don't fall in line. When professors are brave enough to stand out and prepare preservice teachers the way they should be, often preservice teachers step into a school system that is very different than the way they are taught in class. Professors are ridiculed and at times shamed for their beliefs.

Professors are not always invited to speak about what is best for schools. As a democratic community, we should always have an organized, well-represented diverse group when making decisions. Yet companies with money interests in mind seem to have the floor for discussion while others are not *really* involved.

While we must value preservice teachers and teachers currently in the classroom, we must also remember the importance of knowing our truth and standing on our foundational beliefs. We must remember that the art of teaching and the appreciation of being taught new knowledge is a cycle that started long before our time. We need to embrace the knowledge that is being shared from all sides and give value to those who have devoted their entire lives to make sure that education continues.

SUMMARY CHALLENGE

The purpose of this chapter was to revisit the philosophical ways we prepare teachers to lead in today's classrooms. Future teachers must be prepared differently than before. The next season of teachers will be leading the world in a new direction.

There are misconceptions that teachers are given about their role as a teacher. Teachers feel that it is their job to bear all the burdens that the world is facing. They truly see and deal with all the world's issues since the classroom is a mini version of the outside society.

Teachers must no longer be prepared to think they are alone. The future teachers need to be prepared to face challenges with a strong voice and a dedication to do the right things. Being ready from the start to find and use their teacher voice is the way they will rise above the defeat that engulfs a teacher's mind.

Society must value teachers and who is systematically allowed to step into the role of a classroom teacher. When just anyone is allowed to teach, there are issues with every area of education. Students, teachers, preservice teachers, and those who fight for democracy are all impacted.

Prepared teachers need to have their needs met and not feel alone. Supplies, basic needs, curriculum input and lesson planning freedoms, and self-care are a few of the main places we should start. The next generation of teachers need to be prepared to be bold, firm, smart, strong, and never give up on doing what is best for their students and the future of the world.

Summary Questions:

1. This chapter shared that teachers must be prepared to rise up. What can teacher preparation programs do to help the future generation of teachers be prepared to rise up, find their voice, and use it for the better of education?
2. To prepare teachers for the future, this chapter shares that the value of teachers is made known by who we systematically allow to become a teacher. How has society lowered the standards for who can be a teacher? Why do you think this has happened?
3. This chapter shared that highly qualified teachers are needed in every classroom. When unprepared teachers are in classroom positions students, preservice teachers, and democracy are impacted. What can be done to change this situation when so many classroom teacher positions are unfilled due to the teacher shortage?
4. This chapter shared that often educators and other experts are asked to serve on committees when educational changes are being made. How can we make sure that decision makers and education experts are in constant collaboration about needs?
5. This chapter shared that future teachers need to be supported and know that they are not alone. How can teachers be prepared to know that they should not face all the challenges alone? What should teachers do if there is a need not being met?

References

Avi. (2016). *The fighting ground*. HarperCollins.
Bailey, R. A. (2004). *Conscious discipline*. Loving Guidance.
Coerr, E. (1999). *Sadako and the thousand paper cranes*. Penguin Young Readers Group.
Dahl, R. (2007). *James and the giant peach*. Penguin.
Dewey, J. (1899). *The school and society: Being three lectures*. University of Chicago Press.
———. (1906). *The child and the curriculum* (No. 5). University of Chicago Press.
———. (1909). *Moral principles in education*. Houghton Mifflin Company.
———. (1913). *Interest and effort in education*. Houghton Mifflin Company.
———. (2013). *The school and society and the child and the curriculum*. University of Chicago Press.
Dewey, J., & Dewey, E. (1915). *Schools of to-morrow*. Library Reprints, Incorporated.
Dewey, J., & Small, A. W. (1897). My pedagogic creed (No. 25). EL Kellogg & Company.
Francis, Ali. (2022, June 14). Gen Z: The workers who want it all. BBC. https://www.bbc.com/worklife/article/20220613-gen-z-the-workers-who-want-it-all.
Gaudiano, N. (2022, February 5). One ex-teacher in Memphis said she had 194 students during virtual classes because a colleague quit, and it shows why so many teachers are burned out and fed up. *Insider*. https://www.businessinsider.com/teachers-burnout-staffing-shortage-pandemic-quitting-schools-education-2022-2.
Gershoff, E. T. (2017). School corporal punishment in global perspective: prevalence, outcomes, and efforts at intervention. *Psychology, Health & Medicine*, 22(sup1), 224–39. https://doi.org/10.1080/13548506.2016.1271955.
Gibbon, Peter. (2019, Spring). John Dewey: Portrait of a progressive thinker. *HUMANITIES*. https://www.neh.gov/article/john-dewey-portrait-progressive-thinker#:~:text=Dewey%20believed%20that%20a%20philosopher,as%20a%20way%20of%20life.
Harper, K. B. (2022, June 2). Texas was building a program to find troubled students and prevent school shootings. It hadn't reached Uvalde yet. *The Texas Tribune*. https://www.texastribune.org/2022/06/02/uvalde-school-shooting-student-mental-health-program/.

Hess, F., & Weiss, J. (2015). What did race to the top accomplish? *Education Next, 15*(4).

History.com editors. (2018, February 14). Teen gunman kills 17, injures 17 at Parkland, Florida high school. History Channel. https://www.history.com/this-day-in-history/parkland-marjory-stoneman-douglas-school-shooting.

Hughes. M. & Chamberlain, L. (2021, August 9). School years around the world. Infoplease. https://www.infoplease.com/world/social-statistics/school-years-around-world.

Lowry, L. (2014). *The giver*. Houghton Mifflin Harcourt.

Maslow, A., & Lewis, K. J. (1987). Maslow's hierarchy of needs. *Salenger Incorporated, 14*(17), 987–90.

Maxouris, C. & Christina Zdanowicz. (2022, February 5). Teachers are leaving and few people want to join the field. Experts are sounding the alarm. CNN. https://www.cnn.com/2022/02/05/us/teacher-prep-student-shortages-covid-crisis/index.html.

National Commission on Excellence in Education. (1983). A nation at risk: The imperative for educational reform. *The Elementary School Journal, 84*(2), 113–30.

New economic study finds the U.S. could be losing $2.2 trillion annually due to low adult literacy rate. (2020, September 9). Cison. https://www.prnewswire.com/news-releases/new-economic-study-finds-the-us-could-be-losing-2-2-trillion-annually-due-to-low-adult-literacy-rates-301125978.html.

Schimke, A. (2021, February 8). Jeffco to adopt new reading curriculum, push more uniform approach. Chalkbeat Colorado. https://co.chalkbeat.org/2021/2/8/22272626/jeffco-to-adopt-new-reading-curriculum-push-more-uniform-approach.

Scripps National. (2022, May 26). Grandfather of Texas shooter: I'm sorry. *Scripps National*. https://www.thedenverchannel.com/news/national/grandfather-of-texas-school-shooter-im-sorry.

Simpson, D. J. (2006). *John Dewey* (Vol. 10). Peter Lang.

Simpson, D. J., Simpson, J. C., & Jackson, M. J. B. (2005). *John Dewey and the art of teaching: Toward reflective and imaginative practice*. Sage Publications.

Simpson, D. J., & Stack, S. F. (Eds.). (2010). *Teachers, leaders, and schools: Essays by John Dewey*. Southern Illinois University Press.

Tsuchiya, Y. (1988). *Faithful elephants: A true story of animals, people, and war*. Houghton Mifflin Harcourt.

U.S. Department of Agriculture. (2022 February). https://www.nass.usda.gov/Publications/Todays_Reports/reports/fnlo0222.pdf.

Vygotsky, L. S. (1987). *The collected works of LS Vygotsky: Problems of the theory and history of psychology* (Vol. 3). Springer Science & Business Media. https://www.bbc.com/worklife/article/20220613-gen-z-the-workers-who-want-it-all.

About the Author

Latasha D. Holt is an assistant professor of curriculum and instruction, and the assessment coordinator for the College of Education & Human Development at the University of Louisiana at Lafayette. She received her PhD in curriculum and instruction from Texas Tech University. She holds an MS in reading, special education, and English as a second language as well as a BS in early childhood education from Arkansas Tech University.

For the past 16 years, she has worked with children and families, teachers, preservice teachers, and other members of the educational community to promote education. It is her mission to teach, research, and serve in the field of education bridging theory and practice, promoting culturally responsive teaching, and advocating for the whole child.

www.ingramcontent.com/pod-product-compliance
Lightning Source LLC
Chambersburg PA
CBHW020749230426
43665CB00009B/549